# Old Moniaive, Dunscore and the Ca

Isabelle C. Gow

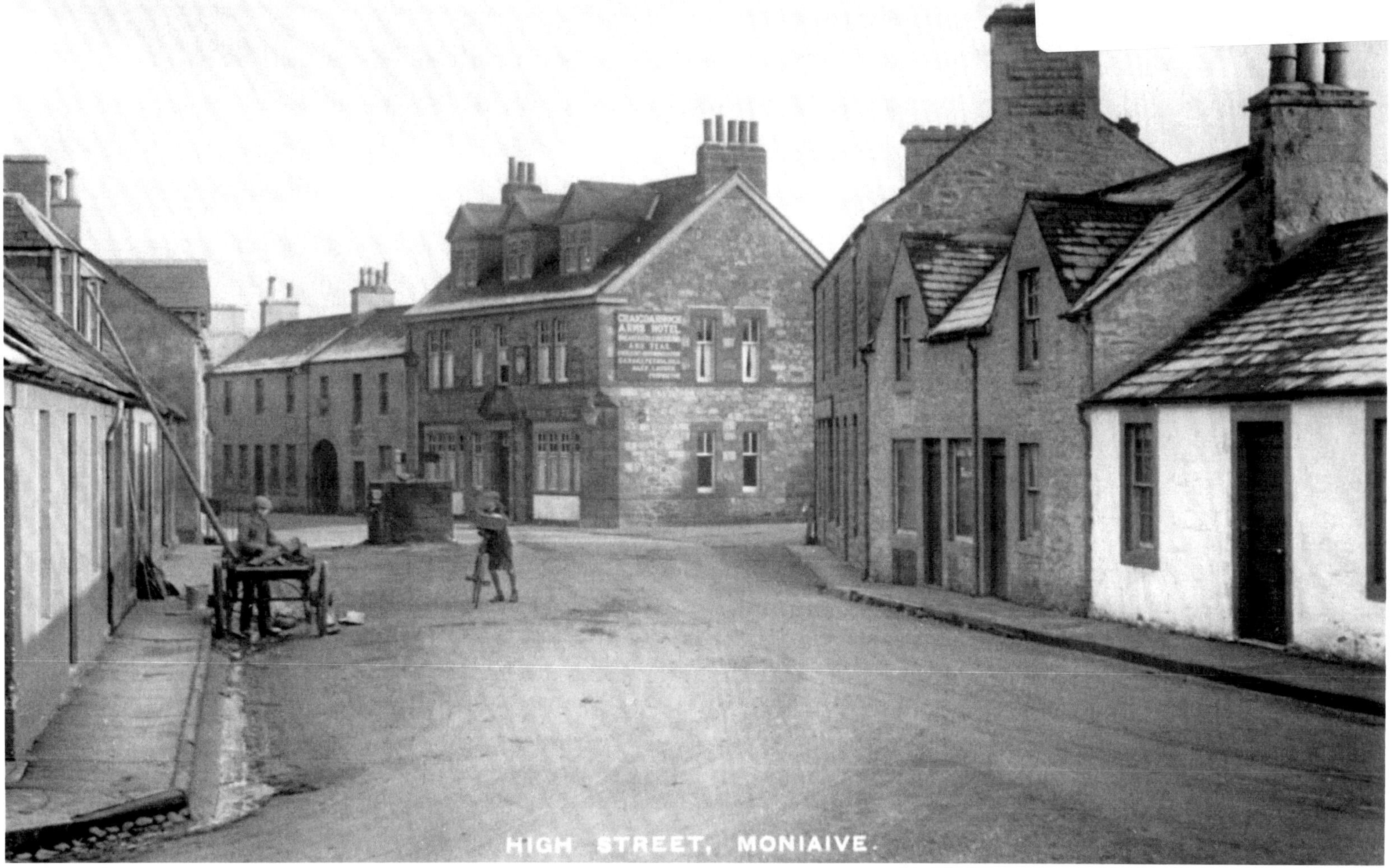

First published in the United Kingdom, 2013,
by Stenlake Publishing Ltd.
01290 551122
www.stenlake.co.uk

ISBN 9781840336344

**The publishers regret that they cannot supply copies of any pictures featured in this book.**

Printed by: Blissetts, West Cross Industrial Park, Brentford, TW8 9EX

## Acknowledgements

With thanks also to Sandy Hall, Frances Dunse, Mary Ritchie and Pam Mitchell for their invaluable local knowledge.

## Bibliography

*Glencairn – the Annals of an Inland Parish* - John Corrie, 1910
*The Cairn Valley Light Railway* – Ian Kirkpatrick
*Story of Moniaive* – Su Palmer-Jones, 1999
*Why Forget?* – Jock Black, 1992
*Dumfries and Galloway's Lost Railways* – Gordon Stansfield
*The Public Roads and Bridges in Dumfriesshire 1650-1820* – James Robertson
*The Story of Dunscore* – Jack Masterton, 1969
*The Parish of Glencairn* – John Monteith, 1876
*Dunscore War Memorial and Parish Memories* – Gladys Cuttle, 2012
*Craigdarroch* – leaflet pub, 1979
*Jane Haining* – Church of Scotland leaflet Revd. David McDougall
*Dunscore Old Graveyard Monumental Inscriptions*, DGFHS, 2005
*Philips Dumfries and Galloway Street Atlas 1939*

Websites
www.moniaive.org.uk; www.dunscore.org.uk;
www.dgnhas.org.uk; www.dunscorechurch.co.uk
www.cwgc.org; www.visionofbritain.org.uk

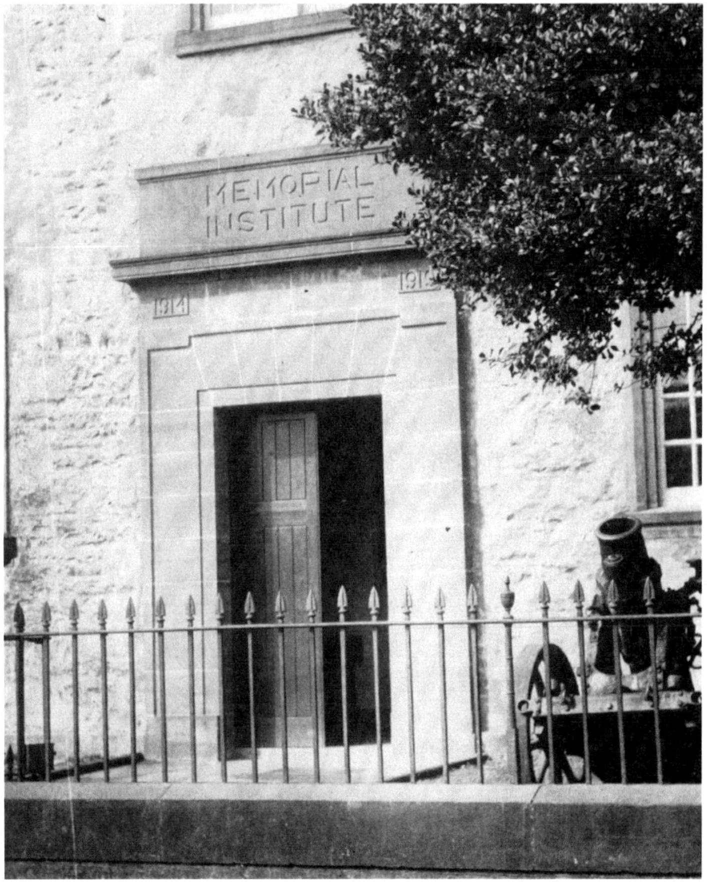


*Above*: The Memorial Institute is situated in Chapel Street, which was previously known as Throughgate. The 1834 building was originally a chapel for the United Presbyterian Church. Shortly after the First World War it was dedicated to the 72 local men, and one woman, who made the ultimate sacrifice in that war. In this street, a soldier of an earlier war, William Smith, lived with his family after he fought at and survived the Battle of Waterloo. Born in Moniaive in 1796 he died in 1874.

# Introduction

Moniaive, Minniehive or Minnyhive is a small picturesque village situated about twelve miles north of Dumfries in the parish of Glencairn between the Dalwhat and Craigdarroch Waters. There has been a settlement here since the 10th century; the mention of a bridge in 1560 reveals that there must have been some sort of community then and in 1636 a charter was granted making it a free burgh with the usual rights to hold weekly markets, annual fairs and have a tolbooth and mercat cross. The burgh has kept its medieval layout of narrow streets and evidence of an earlier way of life can be found in the old street names such as Cow Raw and Mill Raw.

The 19th century saw many villages increase in both population and physical size with the huge expansion of industrialisation common throughout Scotland. Moniaive was no exception and was able to benefit from a gasworks, which was installed in 1861, and a gravitational water supply in 1879. By the mid 19th century there were four churches, two schools, three manses, and a police station. There were millers and blacksmiths, shoemakers and grocers. It had a post office established as early as 1715 and a library, which had been established by 1732.

Today the burgh is thriving. Tearooms and hotels host the annual Folk and Bluegrass Festivals; some well-known musicians, artists, the writer Rumer Godden and more recent celebrities have all made it their home.

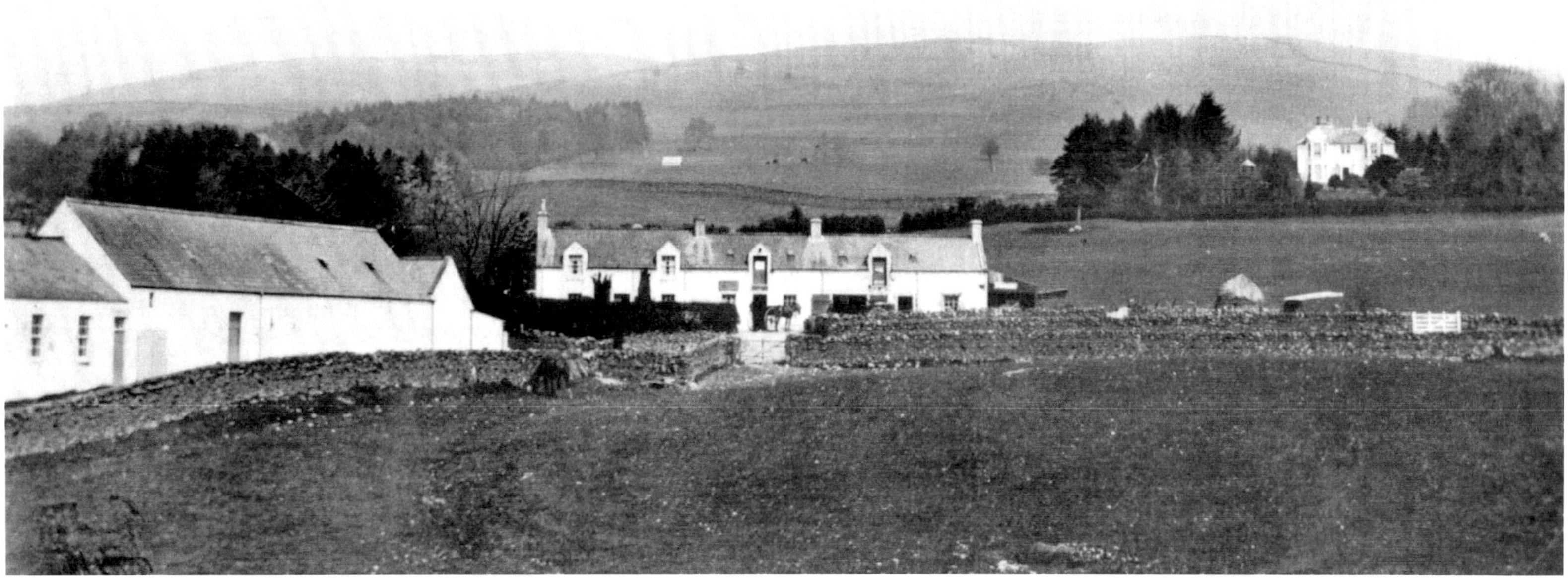

Wallacetown, Glencairn

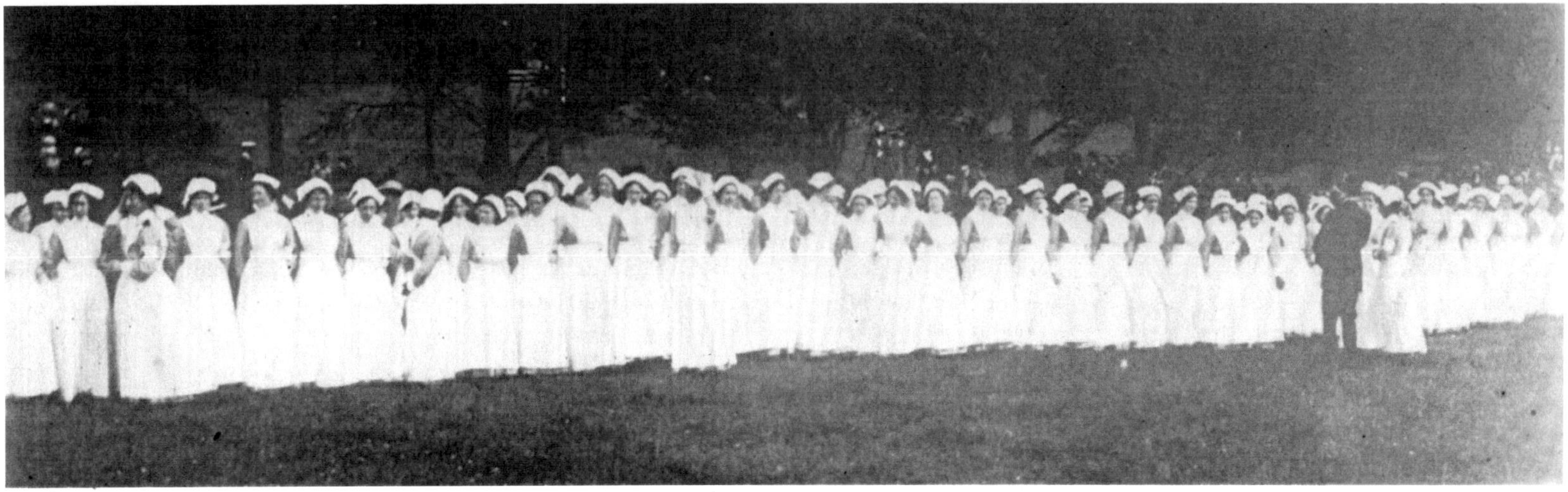

Trained nurses on parade at Glencairn inspected by Sir William Carson on 6th June 1914. These women would soon have to tend to the casualties of the Great War, which was to break out only two months later.

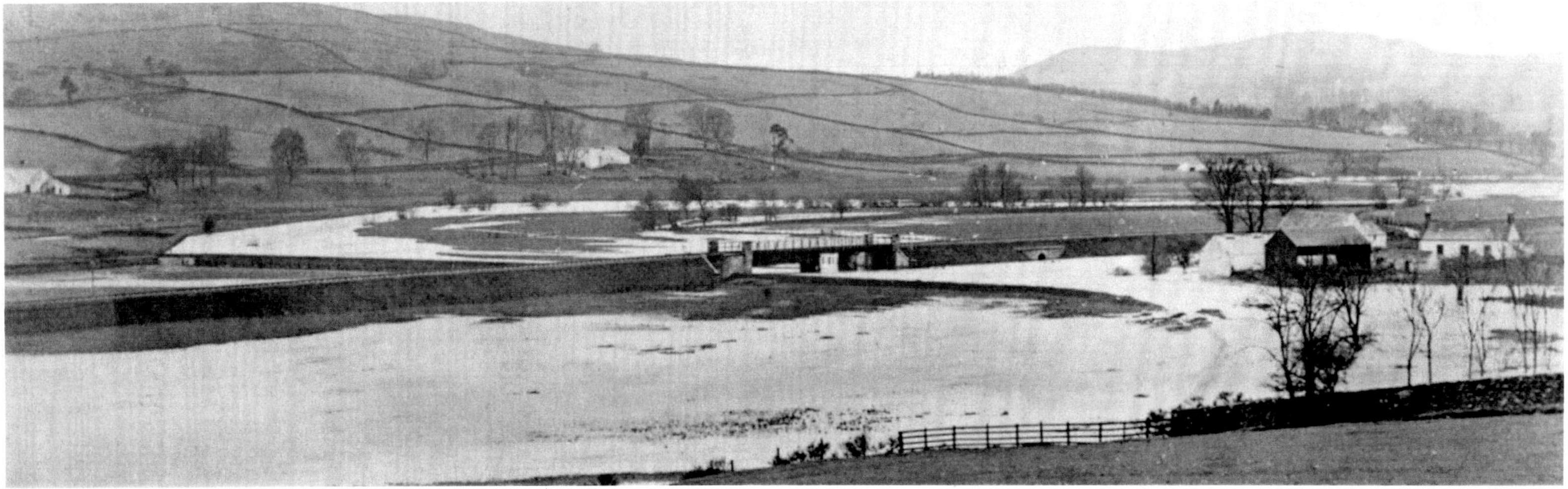

Gaps Mill Farm. Several farms in the district had their own water mills as corn was grown so extensively. In 1914 the farmer was John Gracie although the farm was owned by Captain George L Walker. In the middle distance is the railway bridge over the River Cairn.

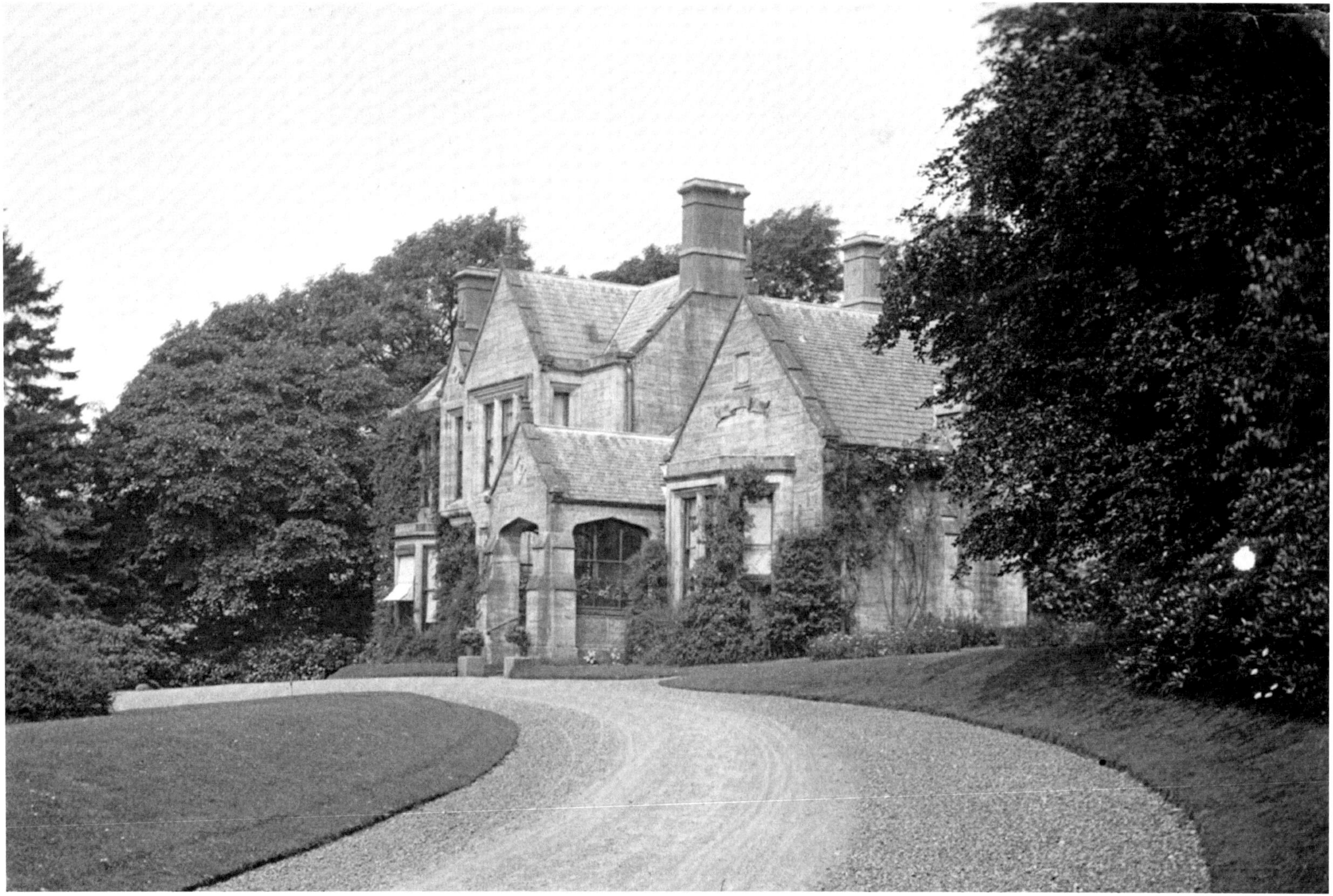

Townhead, Glencairn. The Kennedy family lived here in the early 20th century. Two sons, Lieutenants Walter and Charles Kennedy were both killed in World War One.

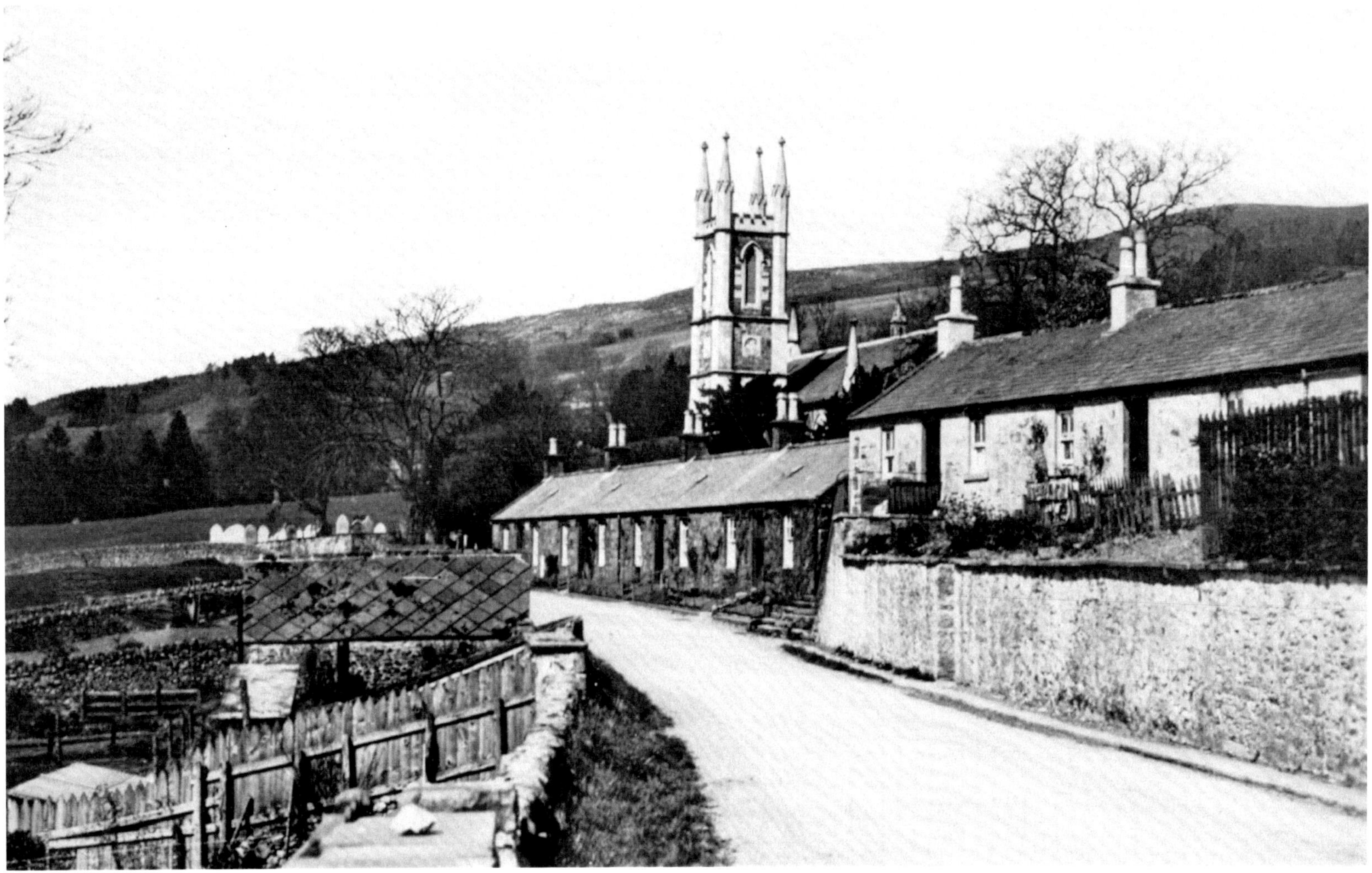

Kirkland Village. Glencairn Church was built in 1836 near the original church. The gables of the pre reformation church survive. In the graveyard there is an impressive red sandstone mausoleum to Gillespie of Peelton; monuments to the Fergussons of Craigdarroch and also slabs inscribed with the names of Covenanters. Reputedly, St Cuthbert visited and worshipped here in the 7th century. The two storey parish manse was designed by the Dumfries architect, Walter Newall in 1840.

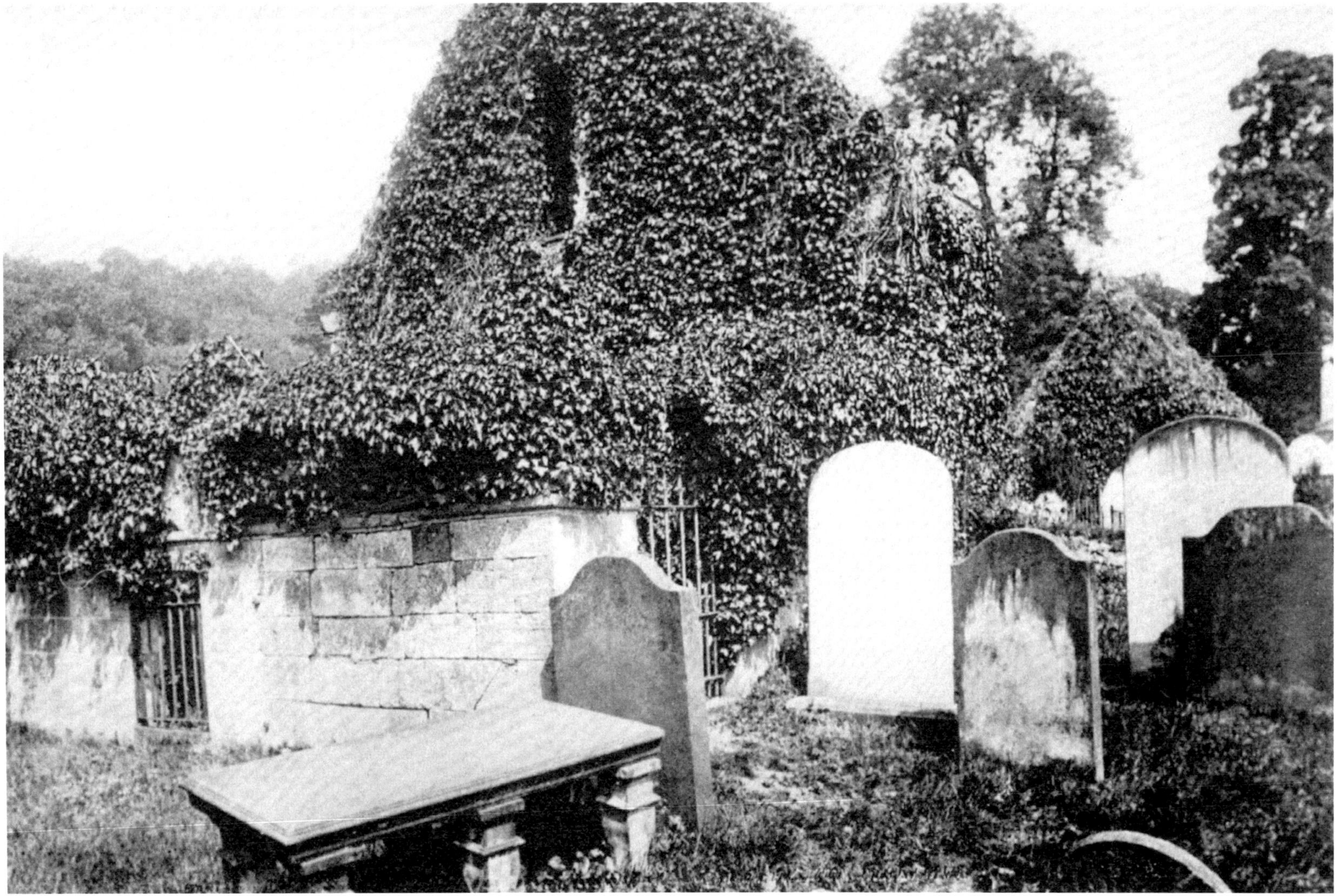

Glencairn Churchyard is supposedly the resting place of Annie Laurie who had lived at Craigdarroch House and died at Friars' Carse, near Auldgirth, in 1763. Just visible are the gable ends of the earlier church. This card by Valentine is dated 1904.

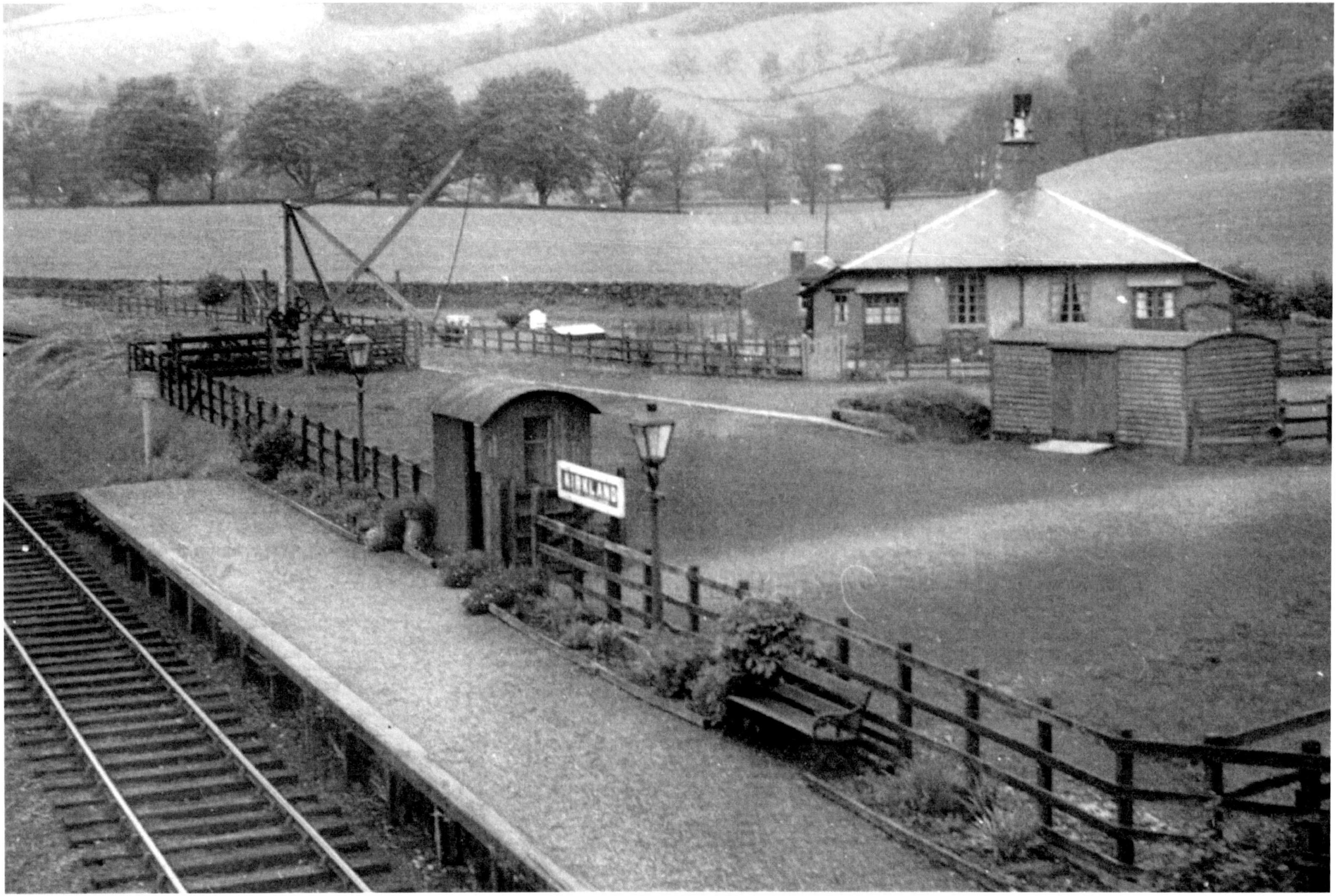


Kirkland Station. The Cairn Valley Railway was opened on 1st March 1905 by a Mr Beattie who had lost both legs in an accident during the building of the line.

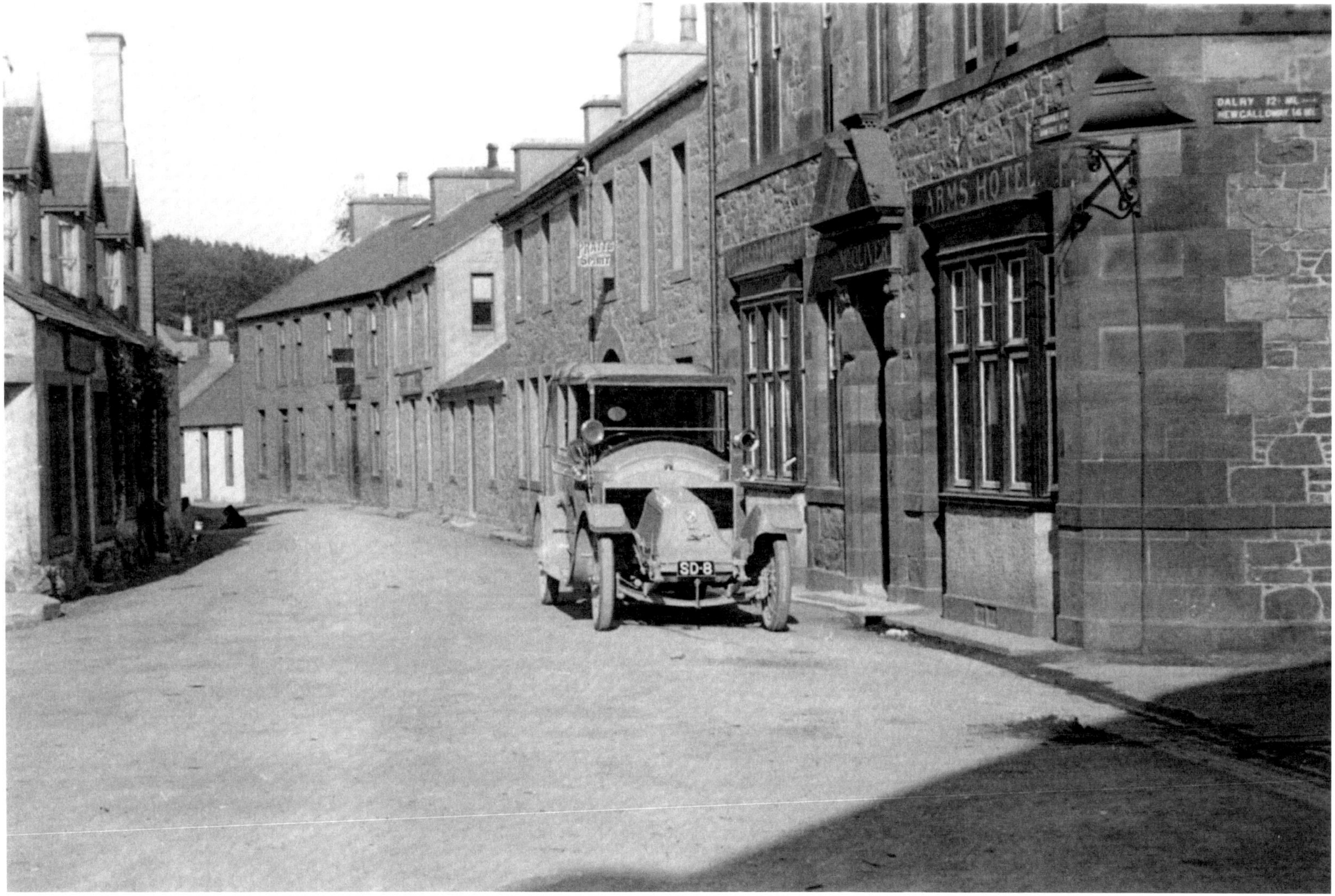


The 19th century Craigdarroch Arms Hotel, the front of which was extended by taking over Macara's grain store. In 1914 the hotel keeper was a widow, Catherine Jane Oliver.

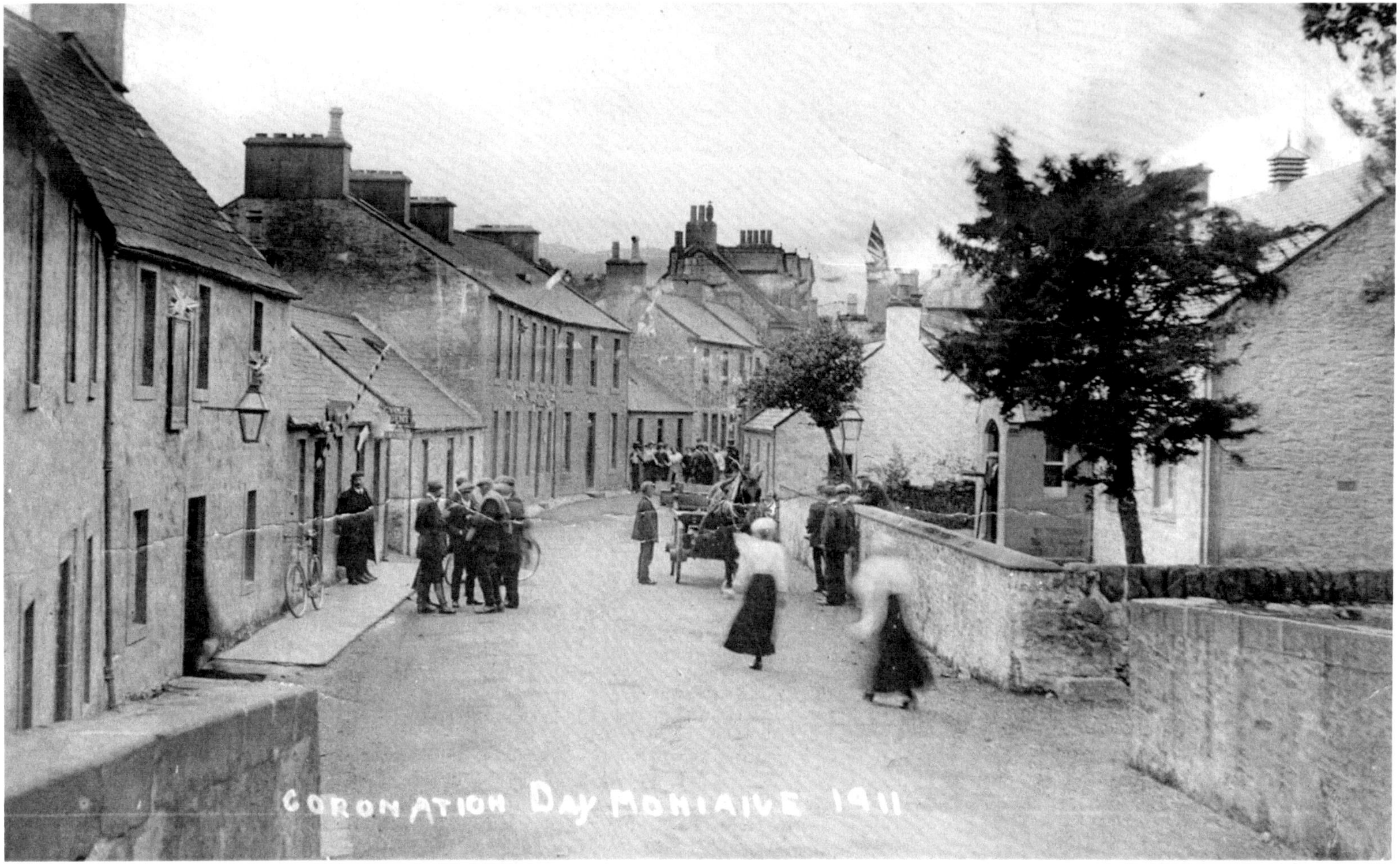


Moniaive on Coronation Day 1911, when George V was crowned king. The flags are flying and the bunting is on display. This view is from the George Hotel at the bridge. The bridge over Dalwhat Water connecting the village to Dunreggan is one which replaced an old arched bridge. Dunreggan was originally the Cow Raw or Cowgate. William Stewart produced a report on the bridge in 1792 after severe flood damage and concluded that it was not worth repairing; goods had to be unloaded from carriages in order to cross it as it was so steep, narrow, liable to further damage in high floods and the pillars being built of whinstone were difficult to repair. He estimated he could build a new bridge at the cost of £200! Payment was completed in 1802.

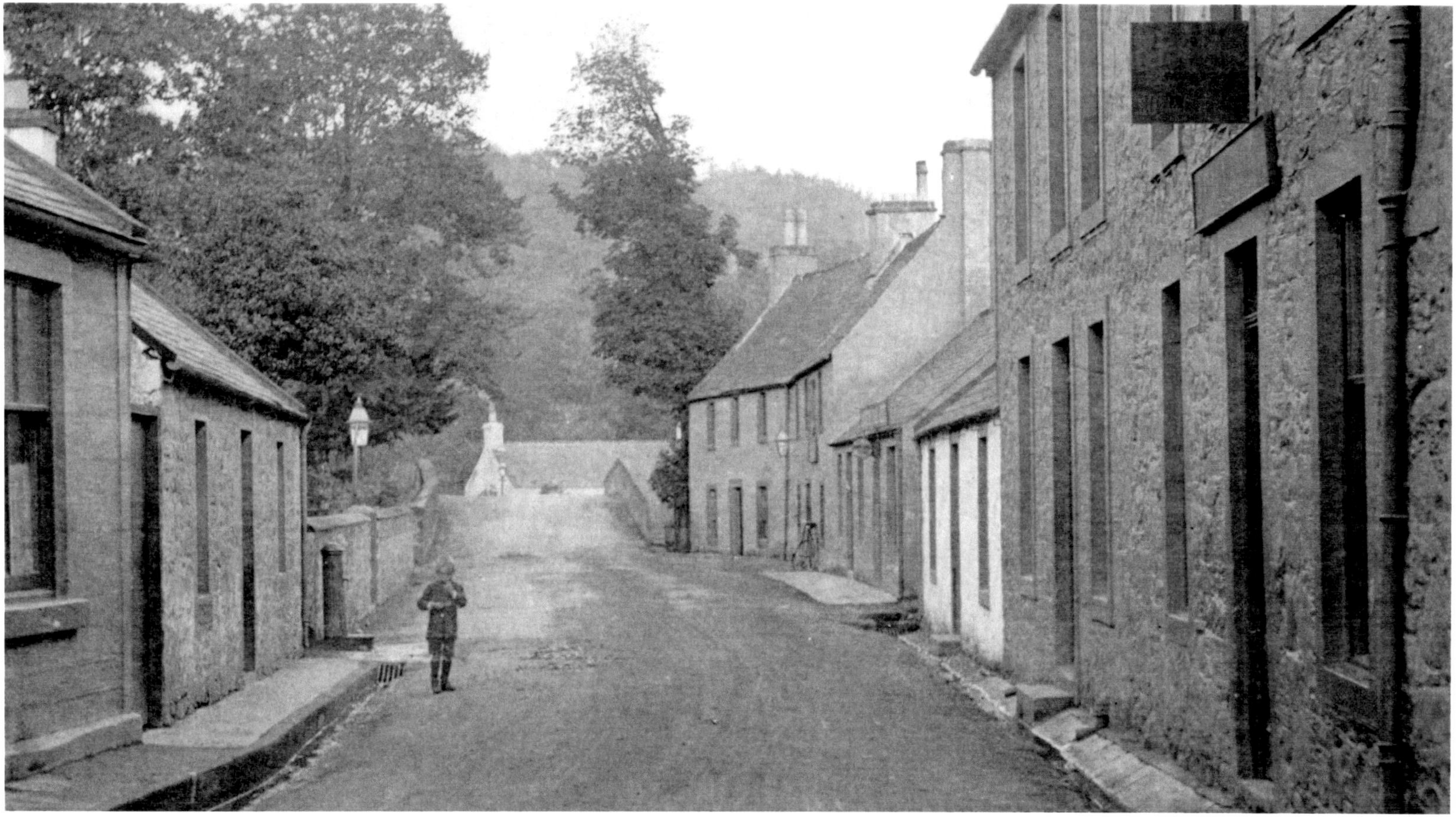

The High Street was originally called the Causey or Causeway at a time when the road was paved with cobblestones. The stones were removed around 1896 to help in the relaying of the village's water channels. Here fairs would have been held in June and September with booths and stalls. Later the fairs were held in a field east of the Free Church and this field became known as Lamb Fair Park. There were tailor and grocer shops; Willie Beattie was the watchmaker; McNaught had a shoe shop; Callander had a store; William Fergusson had the butcher shop with its own slaughter house and Ruth and John McCheyne ran the post office with a telephone exchange, from Westfield House. The family also owned a guesthouse called Sheiling House. McCheyne's cycle store was situated where the post office is today. It had a large doorway to the side to accommodate the handcart and the postmen's bicycles. Five full time postmen were needed in the early years of the 20th century. Mail was collected from Moniaive Station until 1943 when passenger services finished and the bicycles were no longer needed after 1961 when the sorting process was transferred to Thornhill.

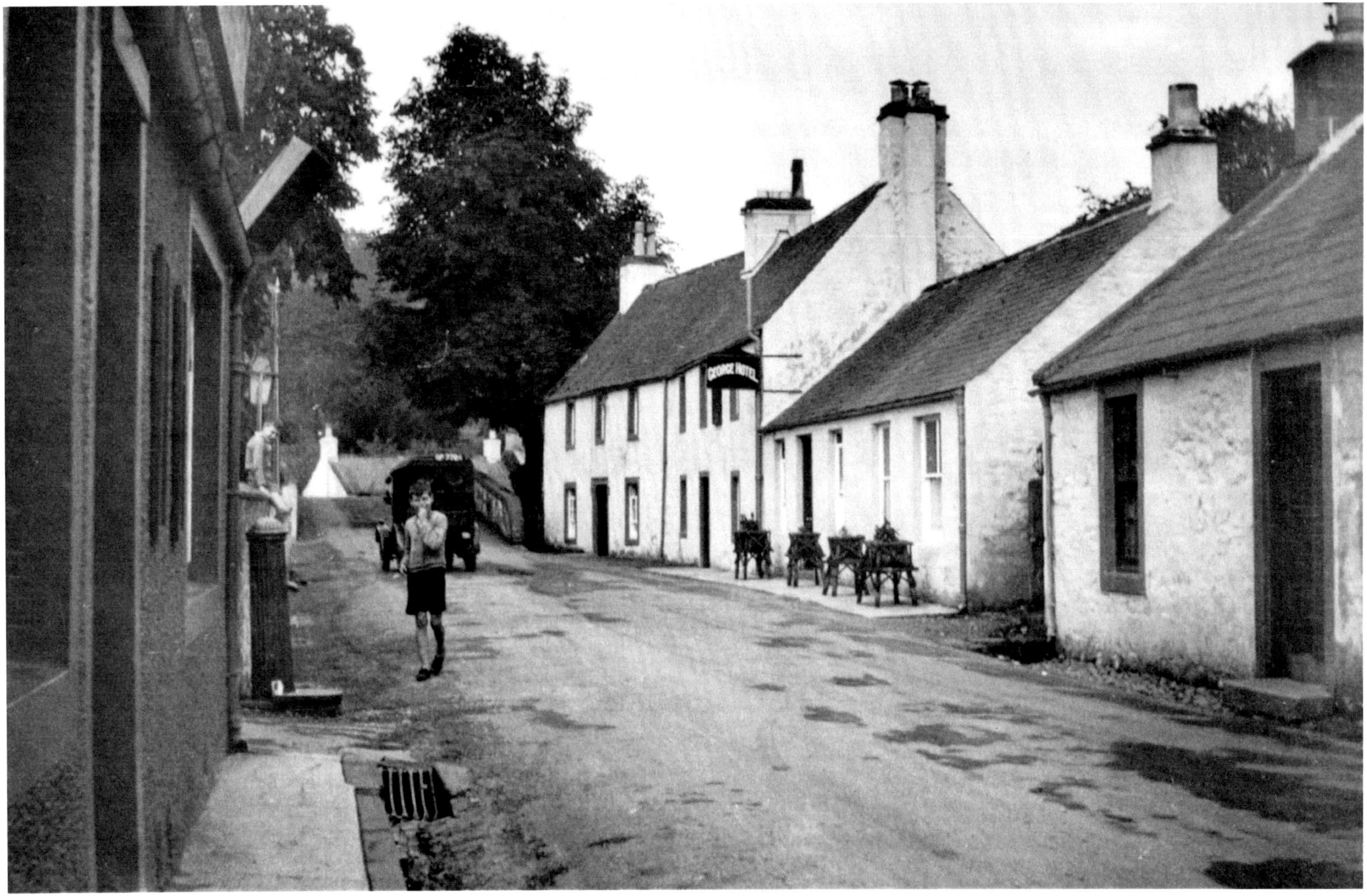


The High Street from the east. The George Hotel, on the right of the photograph, is one of the oldest hotels in Scotland. It was named the George in the 18th century possibly after George III and still has a "Tramps' Hole" so-called as it was where folk left food and drink for vagrants. In 1914 the innkeeper was William John Moon. The family was still there by 1935. Note the water pump on the left of the photograph.

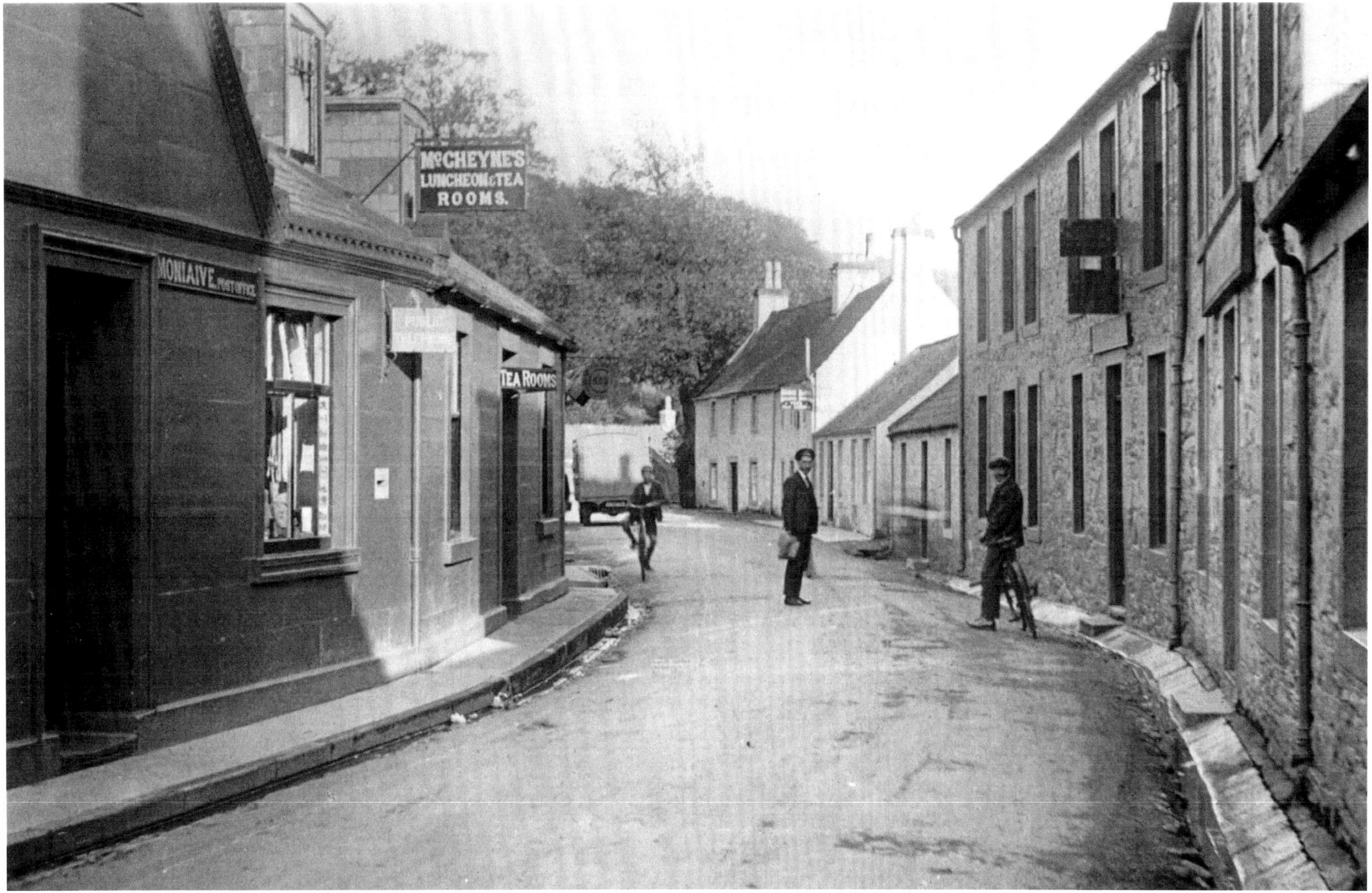


The High Street with the post office, McCheyne's Luncheon and Tea Rooms and the public telephone. The earliest record of a Moniaive postmaster is Robert Davidson in 1768. In the 1841 census the postmistress was Margaret Collow. That was the year after the universal penny post and postage stamps were introduced and the Penny Black appeared.

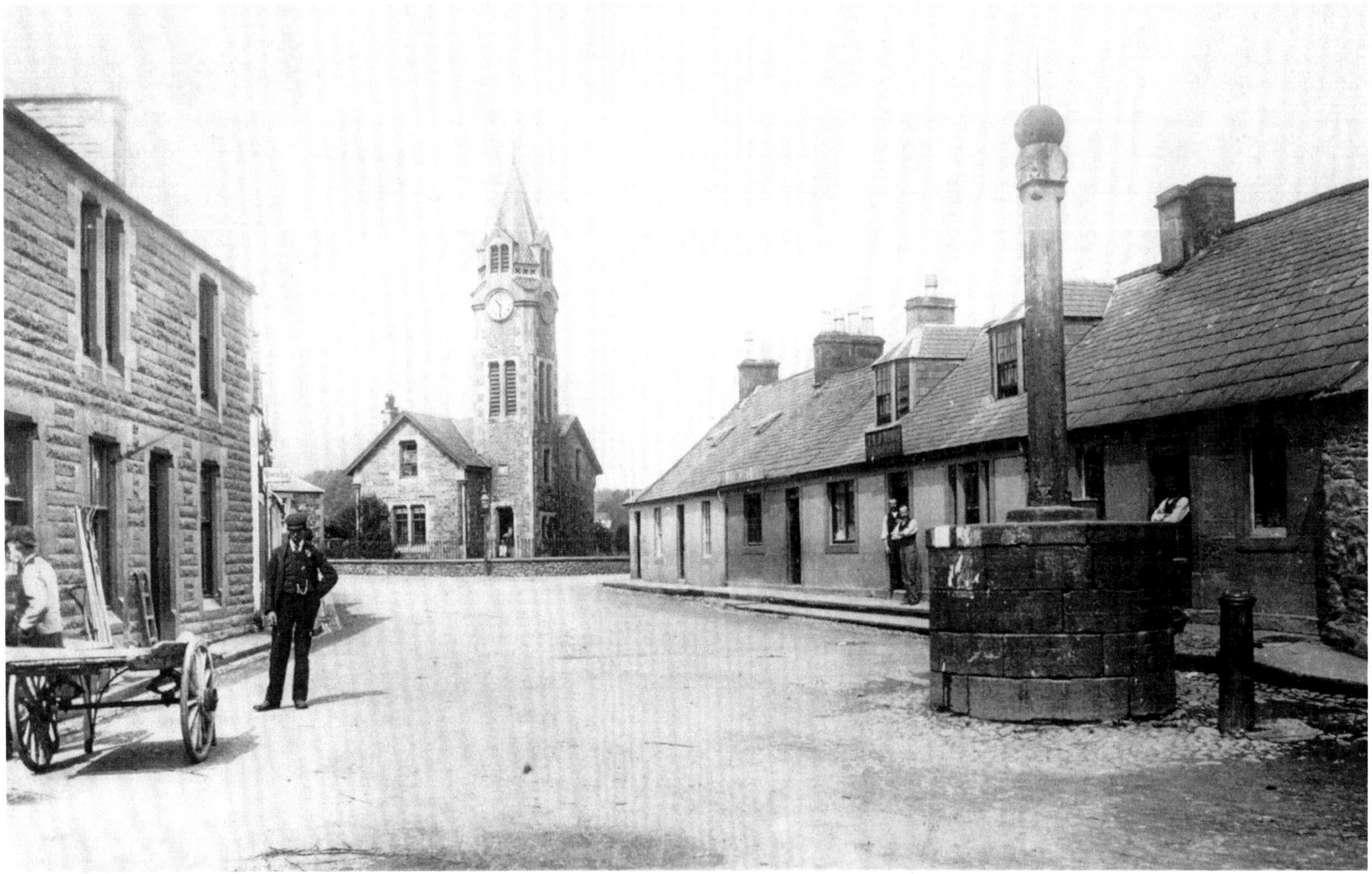

The red sandstone mercat cross on the High Street was erected in 1638. It originally had a sundial on top and a square base. The stone ball is a 19th century addition. The "jougs" (stocks attached to the base of the cross) were removed in 1812 and can be seen in the Memorial Institute. A blind musician, composer and author of some repute, James Fisher, was born in the High Street about 1759. He published several poems and prose writings. His wife is buried in Glencairn Churchyard.

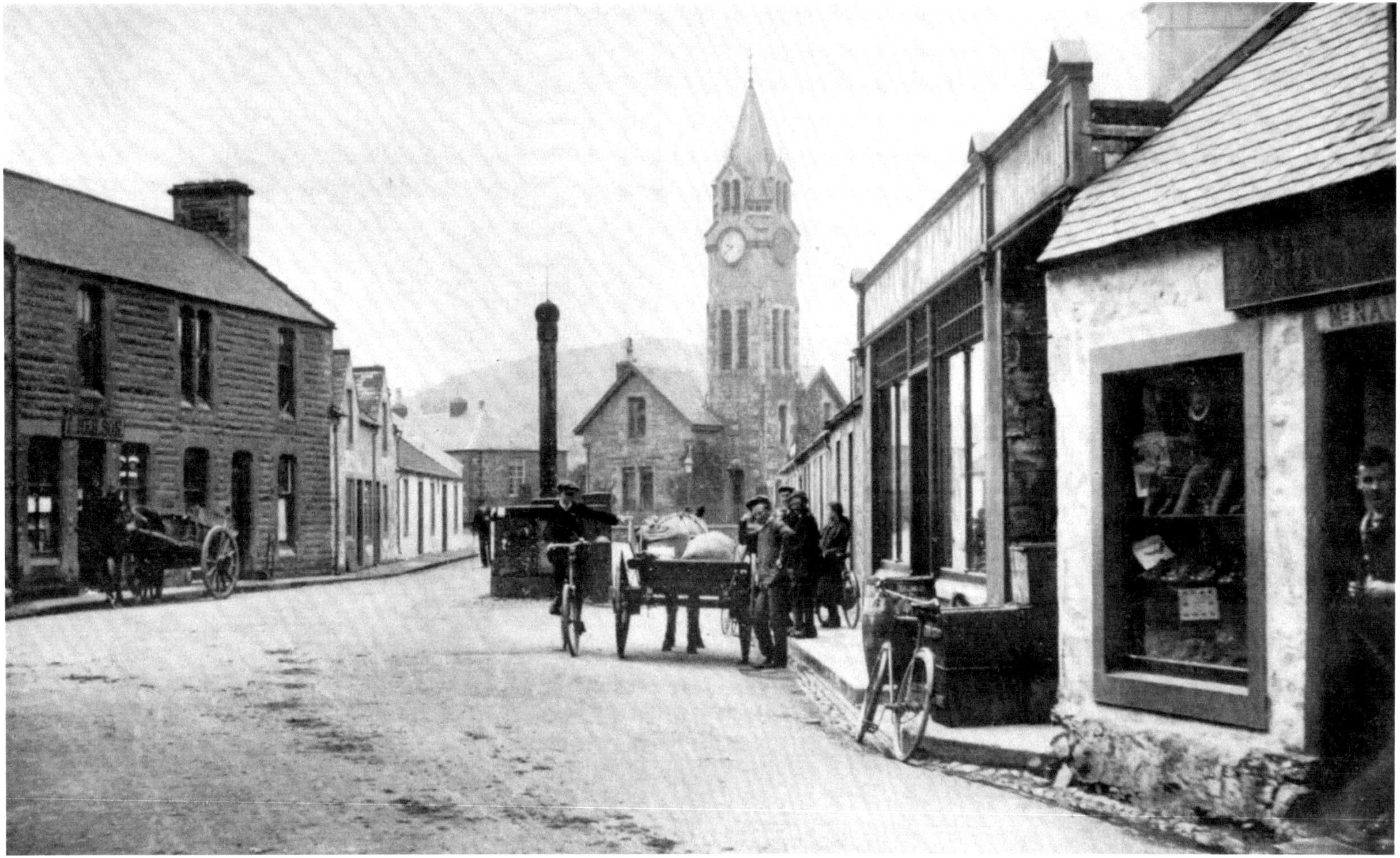

The Mercat Cross, High Street about 1905. In the 19th and early 20th centuries the main forms of transport were the horse and cart, coach and bicycle. In 1833 the Craigengillan Coach began to run between Dumfries and Glasgow calling at Moniaive. Then in 1865 the Moniaive Omnibus Company was formed to run between Moniaive and Thornhill. This continued until 1905 when it was abandoned soon after the opening of the Cairn Valley Railway. The clocktower in the background was the schoolmaster's house. The shop with the double front used to belong to Graham F Macara and is now Watson's. (Macara Park was gifted to the village by this grocer.) Thomas Neilson had his store on the left opposite the cross.

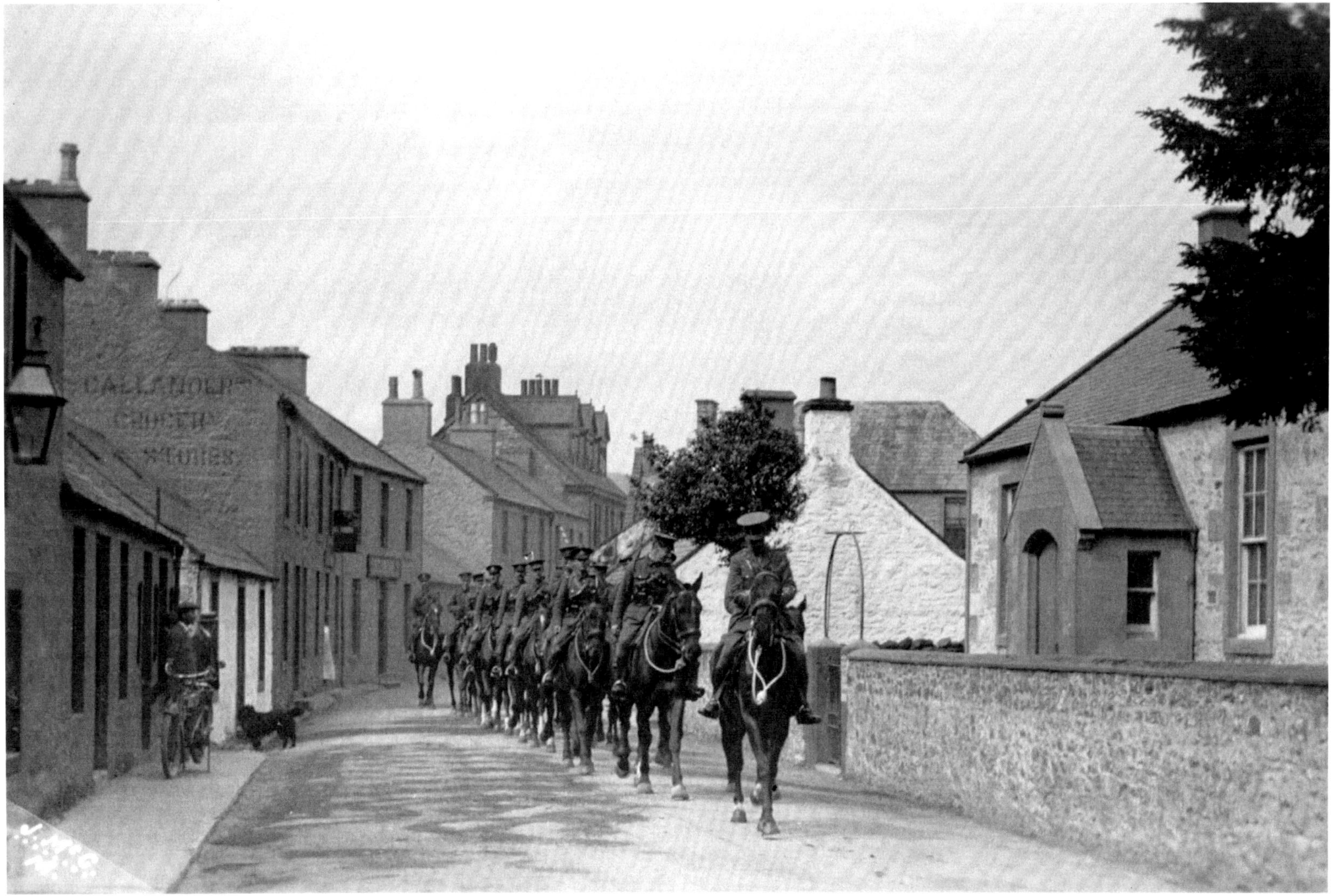

The soldiers on horseback are from the Ayrshire Yeomanry just before the First World War. They are passing the Masonic Hall on the right, which had previously been used as the village hall. On the left on one of the buildings is an advert for Callander's Grocery Store in the High Street.

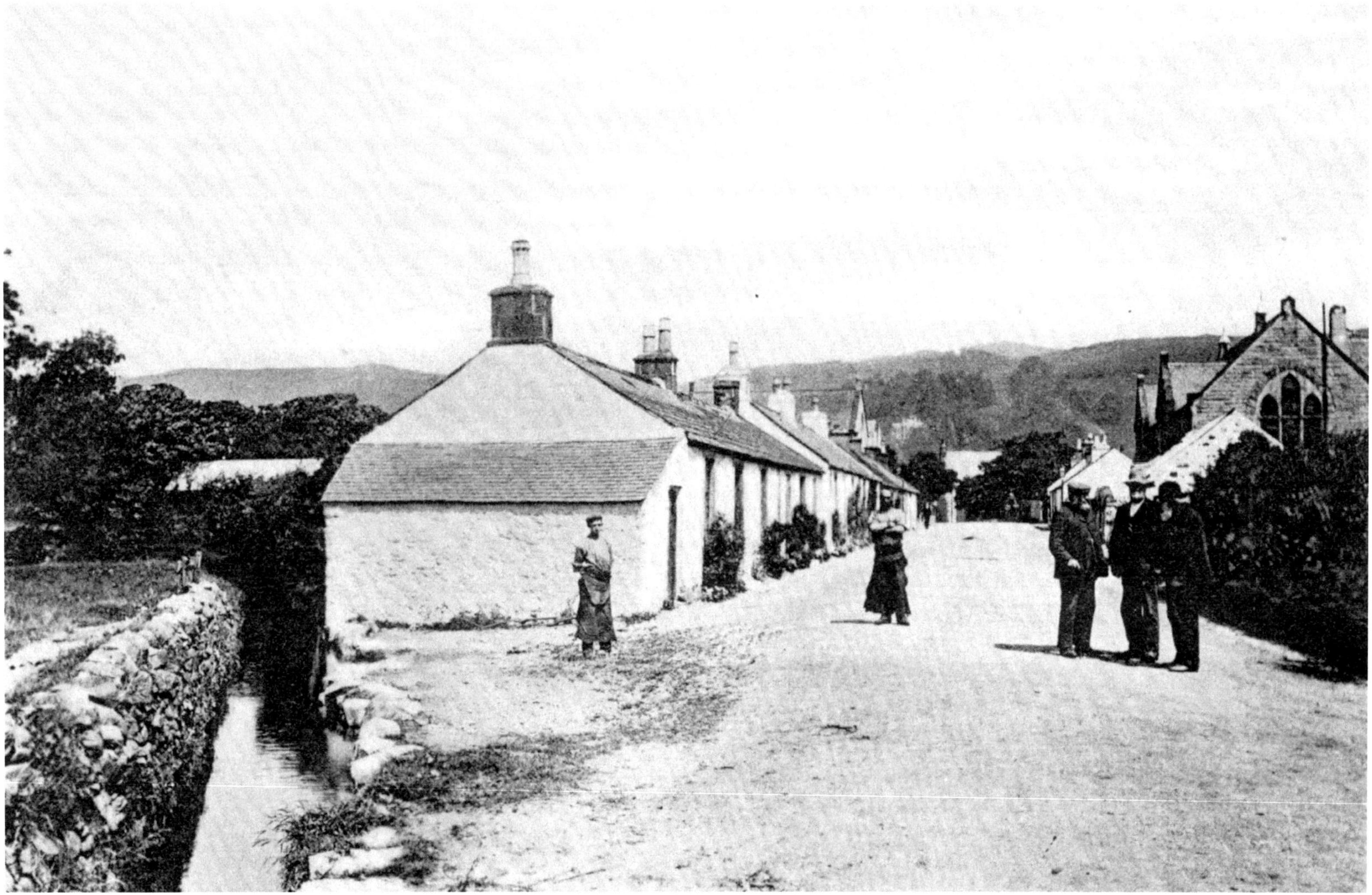

This 1935 view shows the village blacksmiths on Chapel Street one of whom was William Dalziel. It is taken from the New Galloway Road and also shows the mill leet. In 1837 the parish of Glencairn had three parish schools with an attendance of 148 and two female (dame) schools with an attendance of 70. Here in Chapel Street in 1857 a Mrs Barbour had a school erected to house about 100 scholars.

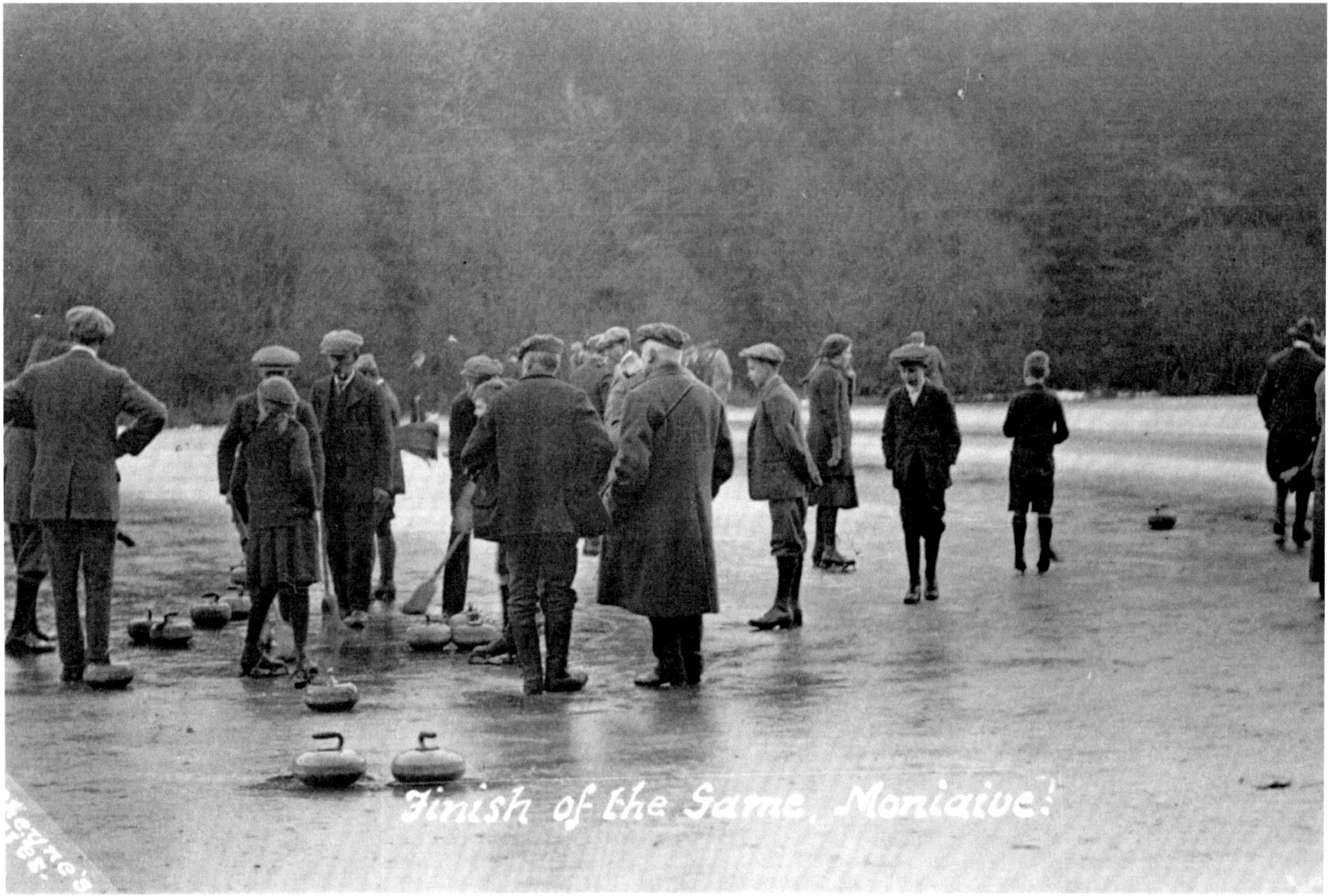


This view dates no later than 1914. There were several curling clubs nearby - at Maxwelton, Barbuie and Two Merkland. Lochs were used as well as an artificial pond capable of accommodating two rinks.

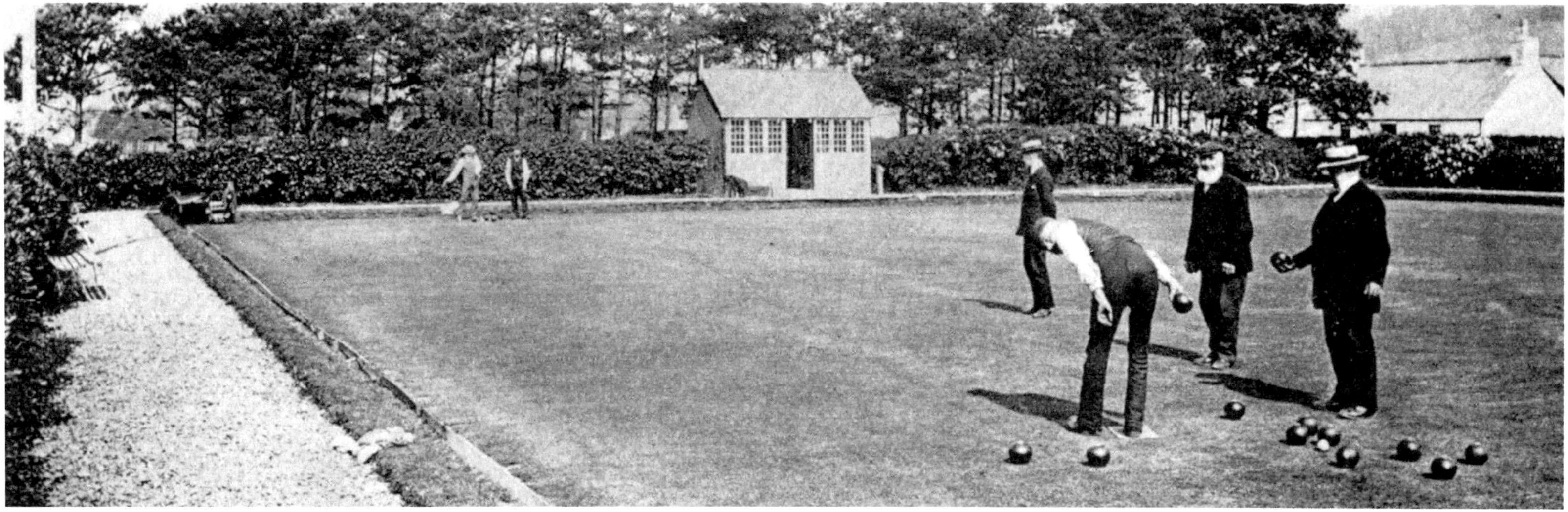

Colonel Walker of Crawfordton gave the land for the bowling green, which was opened in 1870 which still exists, but with a bigger clubhouse. The message on this post card, sent in 1904, reads, "it is only one of the many attractions we have at Moniaive I don't think"!

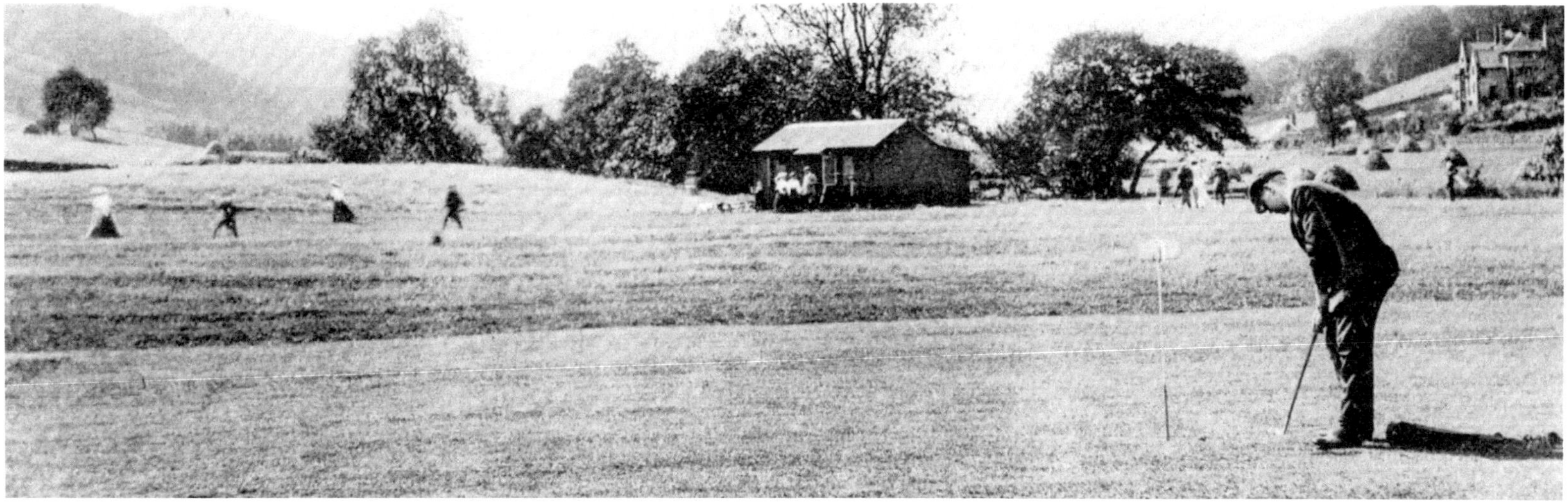

This nine-hole golf course at Crichen opened in 1905, but is now farmland, having been ploughed during the Second World War.

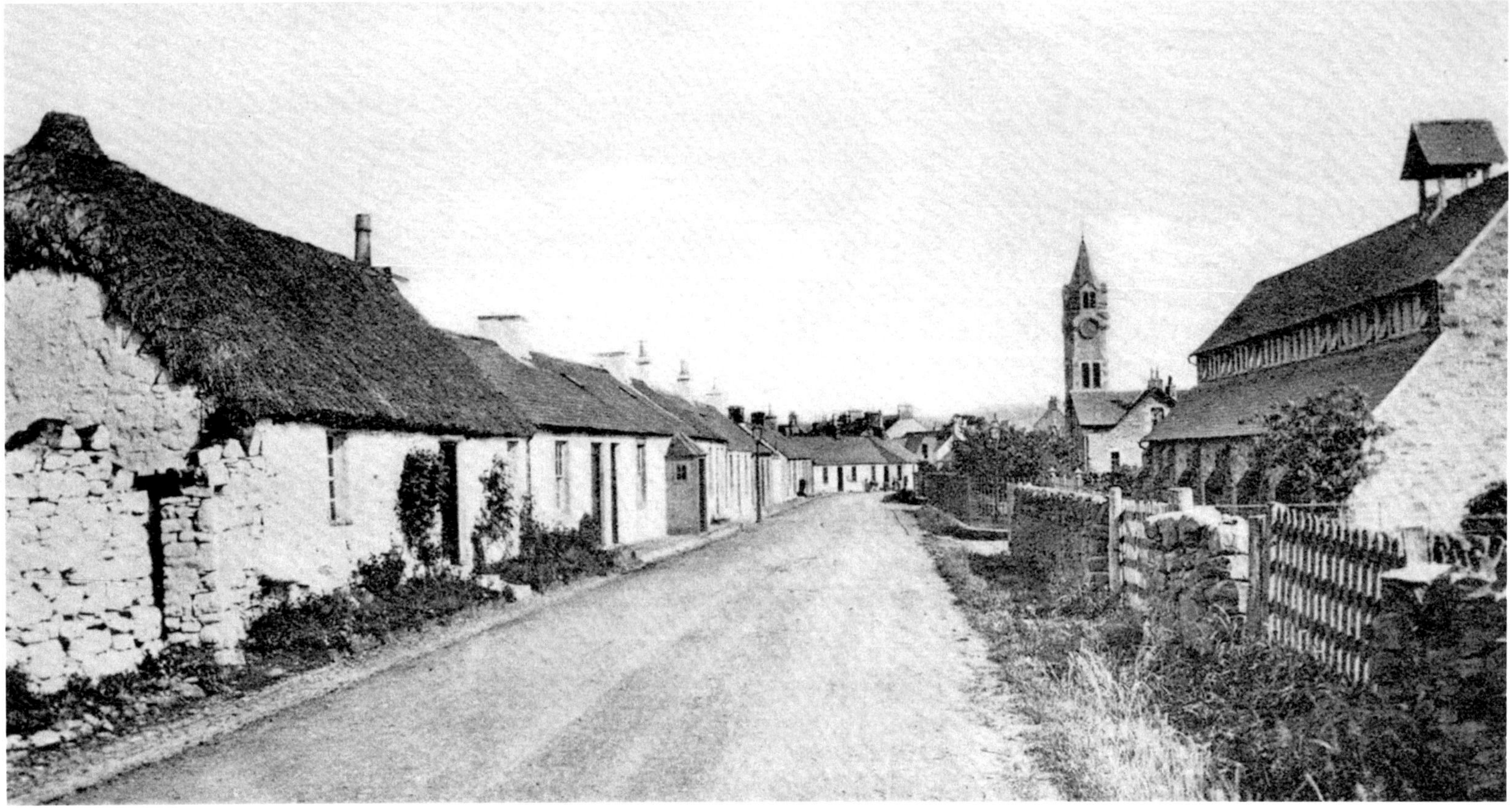

North Street used to be called Beggars' Raw. The old cottage on the left, which was demolished in 1899, had cobble stone floors and a roof of oak branches covered in straw thatch and was the last of its type. Opposite is St Ninian's Church, built in 1887 as a chapel of ease for Glencairn Church at Kirkland. Behind the church was the sawmill. There still exists a painted sandstone building, which was used as hearse house similar to the one in Dunscore. In the distance is the Tower House built in 1865 to accommodate the schoolmaster.

*Opposite*: Ayr Street was once known as Mill Raw after Craigdarroch Corn Mill – later Macara's Mill and renamed Ayr Street after the new turnpike road to Ayr was opened. Amongst the traditional cottages (now preserved) there was a clogmaker called Rutherford and a grocer shop run by the Kennedys, which was then taken over by McCulloch to sell fish. There were two dressmakers, Dalziel's sweetie shop and Swan the blacksmith. The police station (now a private residence) was built in 1865 and included cells. At the top of the street was a lane known as "The Course" – an actual racecourse!

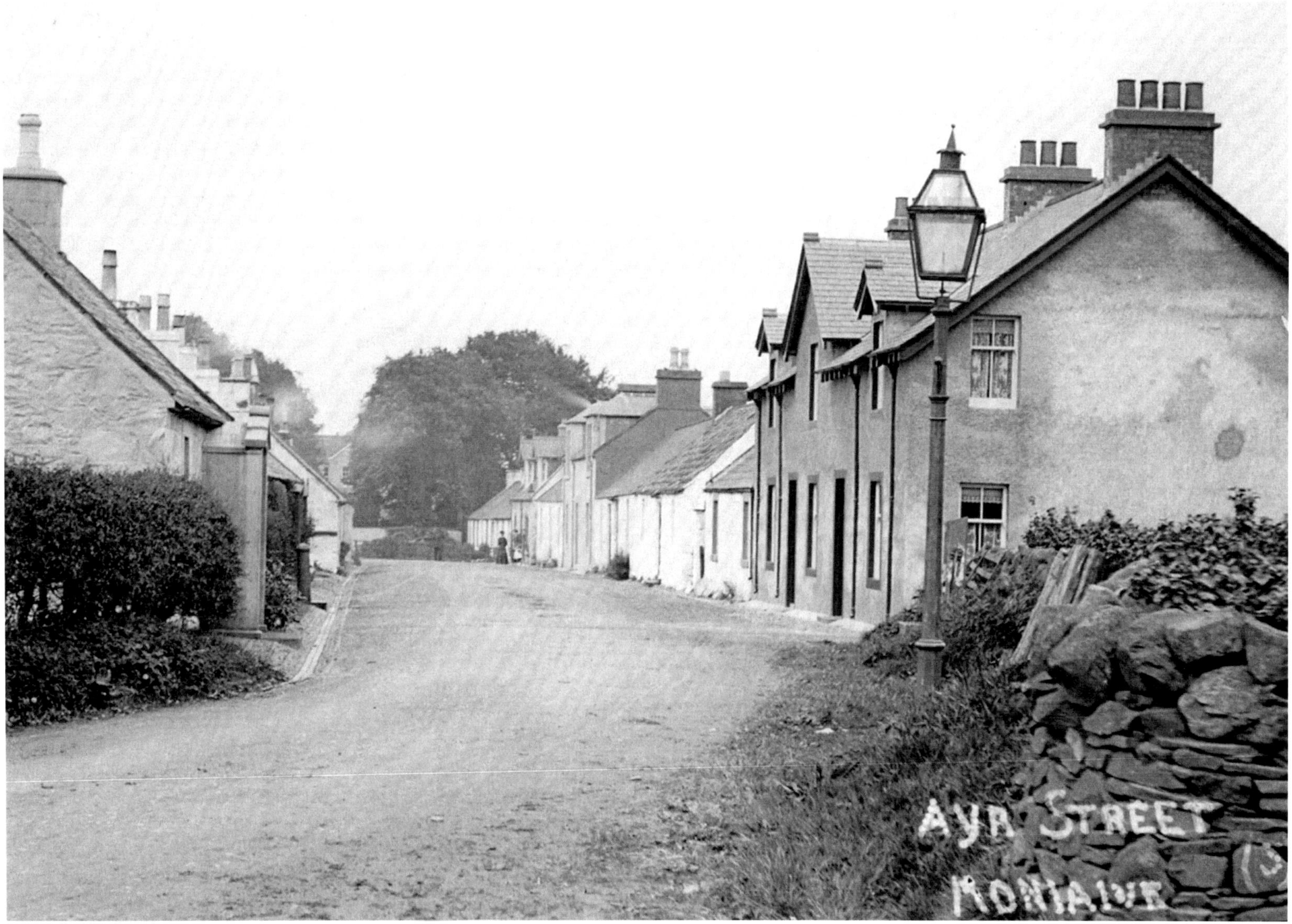
AYR STREET
MONIAIVE

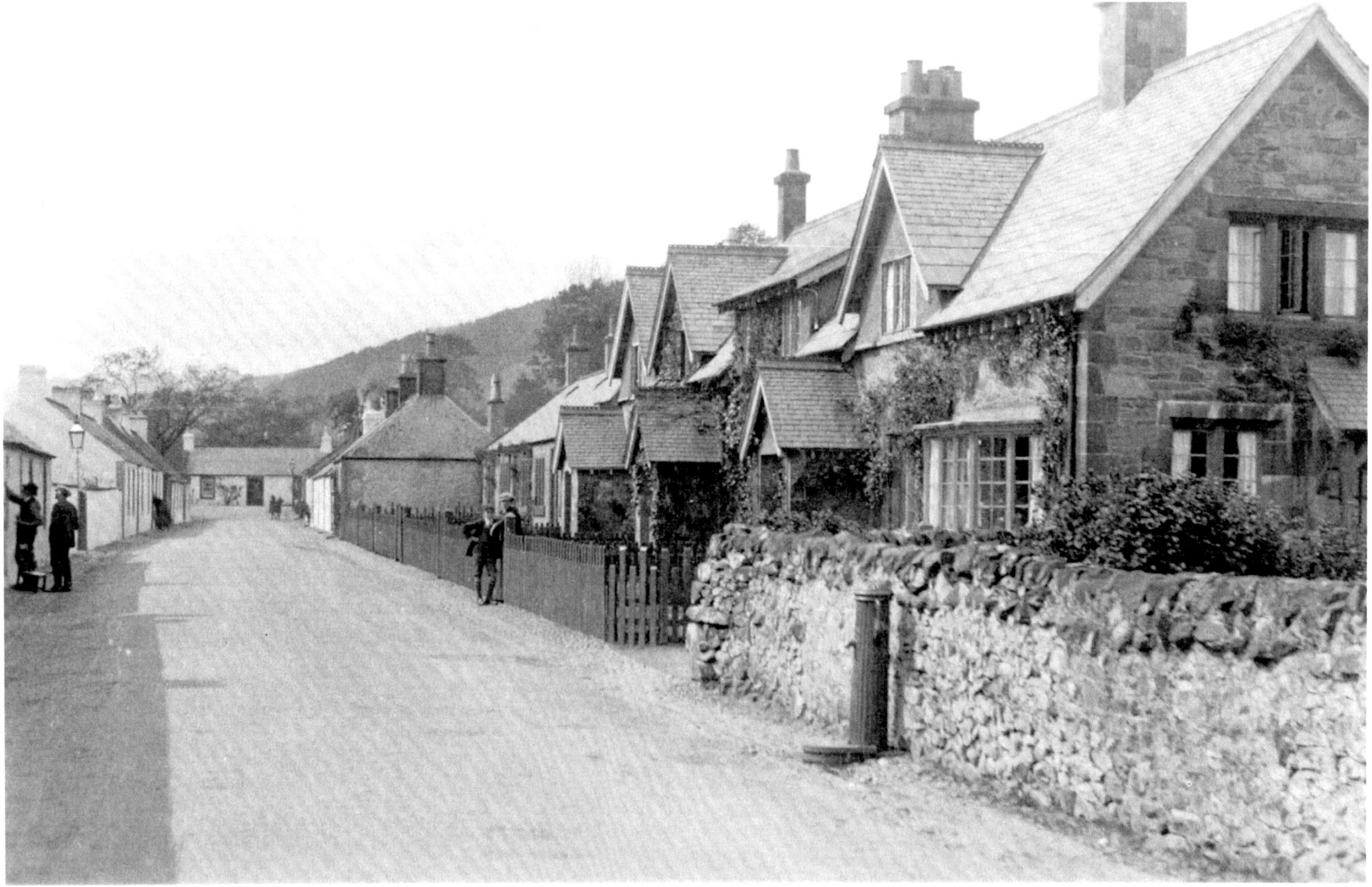

This 1928 postcard shows Dunreggan, which at one time was a separate village. Mrs Menteith had commissioned her brother, the architect, William West Neve, to build her Arts and Crafts Style house, Glenluiart, in 1898. She then commissioned him to build these houses in 1906. They have a date stone with the initials EM. There was a tollhouse and a weighing machine in this street and this was where a school and a jail were also situated.

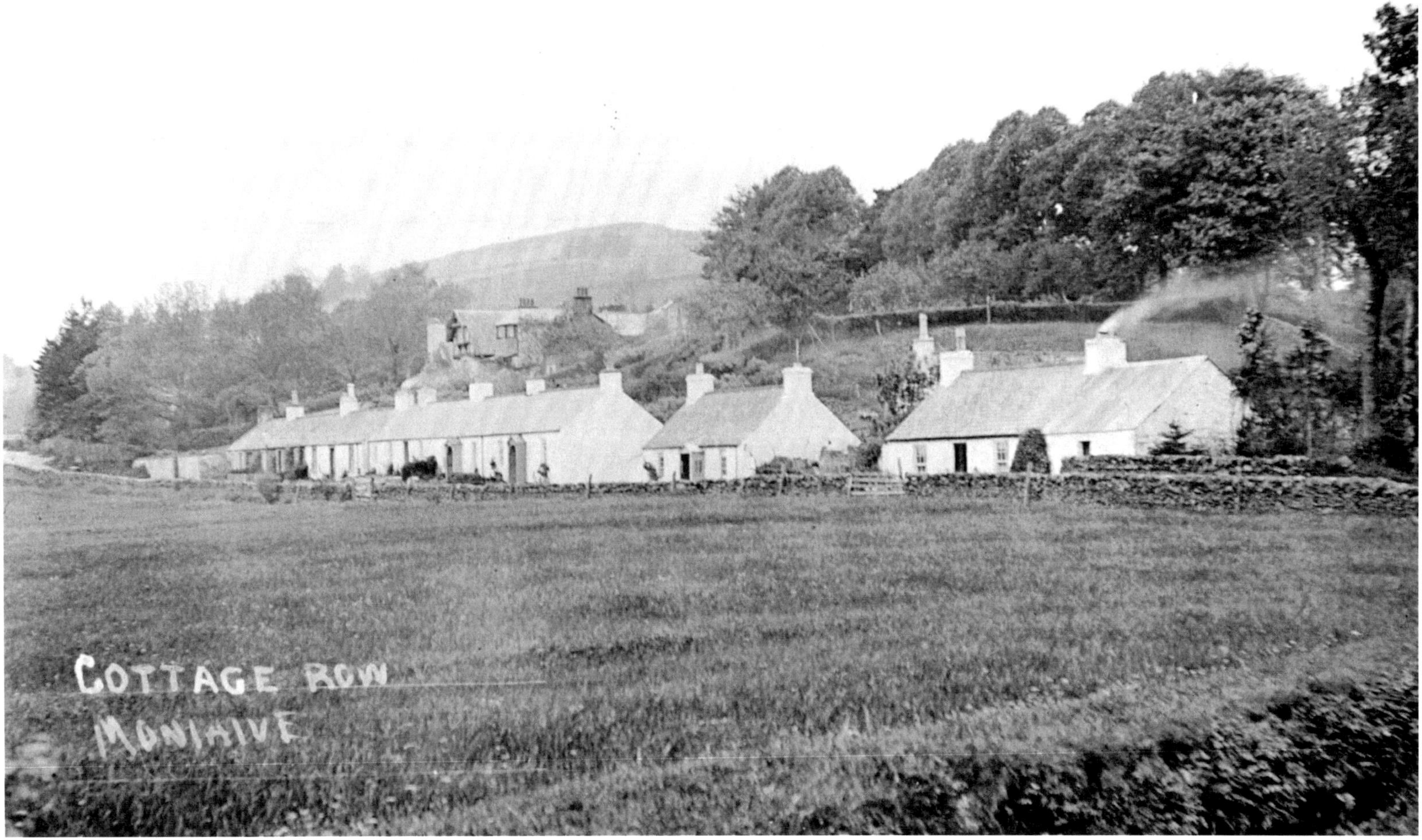


The big house in the background is Kilneiss (Neiskiln on old maps), which was built in 1884 as a wedding present for the artist, James Paterson who was one of the Glasgow Boys. He painted the Craigdarroch Millpond in "The Last Turning, Winter, Moniaive, 1885" (now in the Kelvingrove Art Gallery, Glasgow); the painting "Moniaive" showing the Clock Tower and the "Craigdarroch Mill" which was painted in 1882 from Cottage Row.

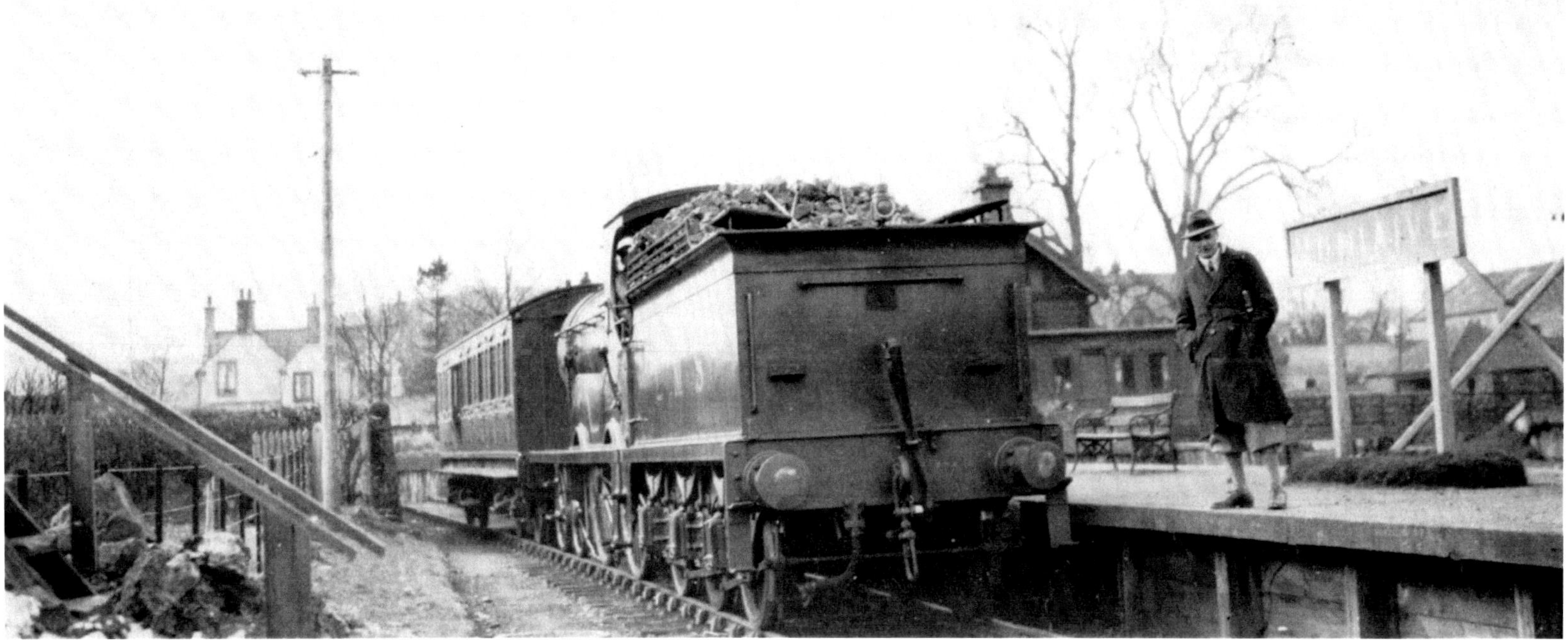

Moniaive Station in 1934. The line from Moniaive to Dumfries was a 16-mile line run by the Glasgow and South Western Railway Company and opened in 1905, however the passenger service ceased in 1943. It had served, Moniaive, Kirkland, Crossford, Dunscore, Stepford, Newtonairds and Irongray. The station had its own house, and an engine shed which still remains near Chapel Street. The last employees were Mrs Jean Marchbank and Harry Sutherland. The old post office was conveniently across the road. Nearby was the Waulkmill Blanket Mill owned by Willie McCaw. The blankets had a small black and red regular square pattern. The censuses of the mid 19th century list several dyers amongst the occupants of the village, but by 1914 the mill stood empty. Grains Road used to be known as The Stenters and was the place where the cloth would have been stretched out with stenters (poles) near the Waulkmill.

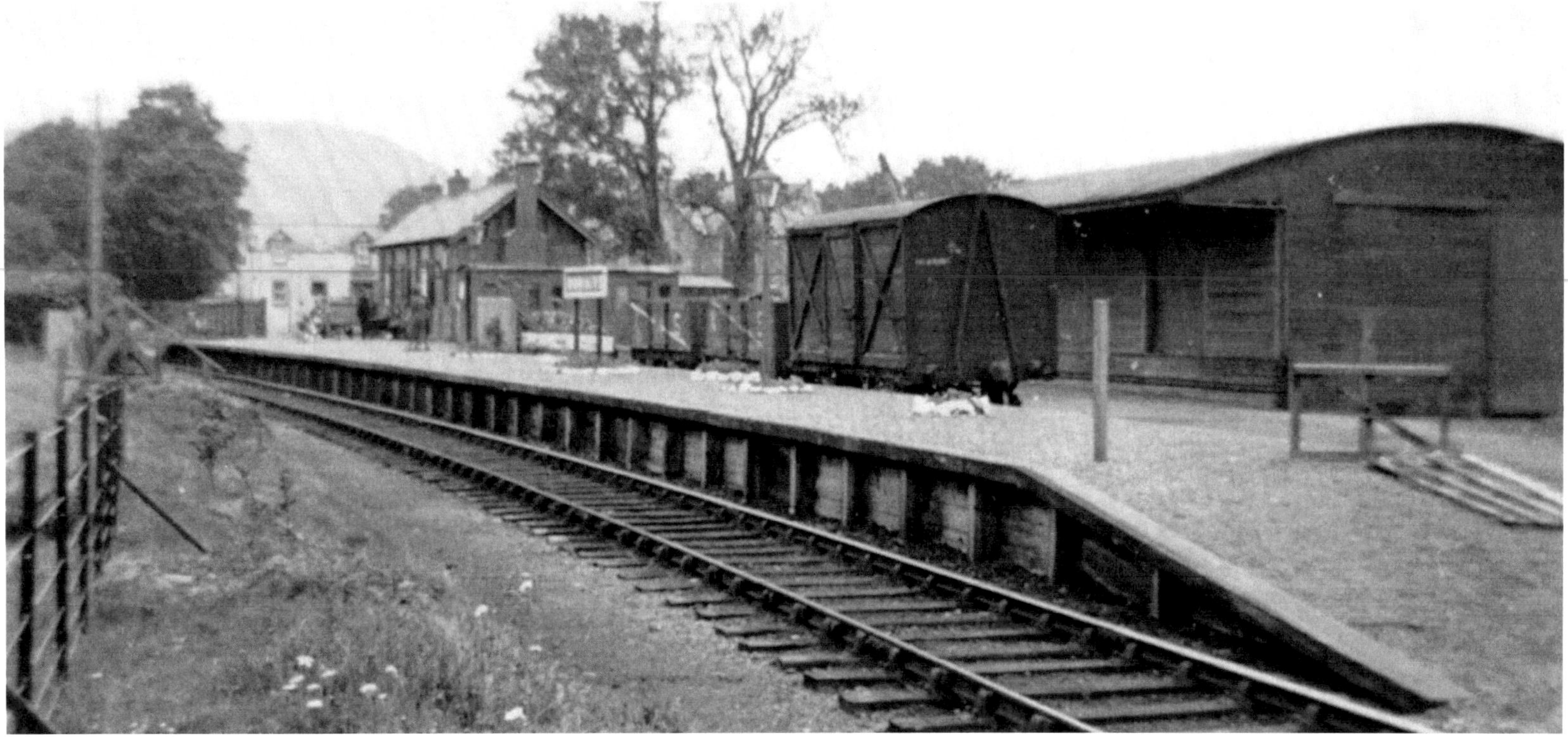

A poem was written to acknowledge the opening of the railway line:

The farmers frae amang the hills,
At last a chance will hae,
To get their stock into the toon,
Upon a market day.

In fact along the glen ye'll fin'
That every ane will thrive,
Noo that the line is opened
Frae Dumfries to Moniaive.

Taken from "The Story of Dunscore", Jack Masterton.

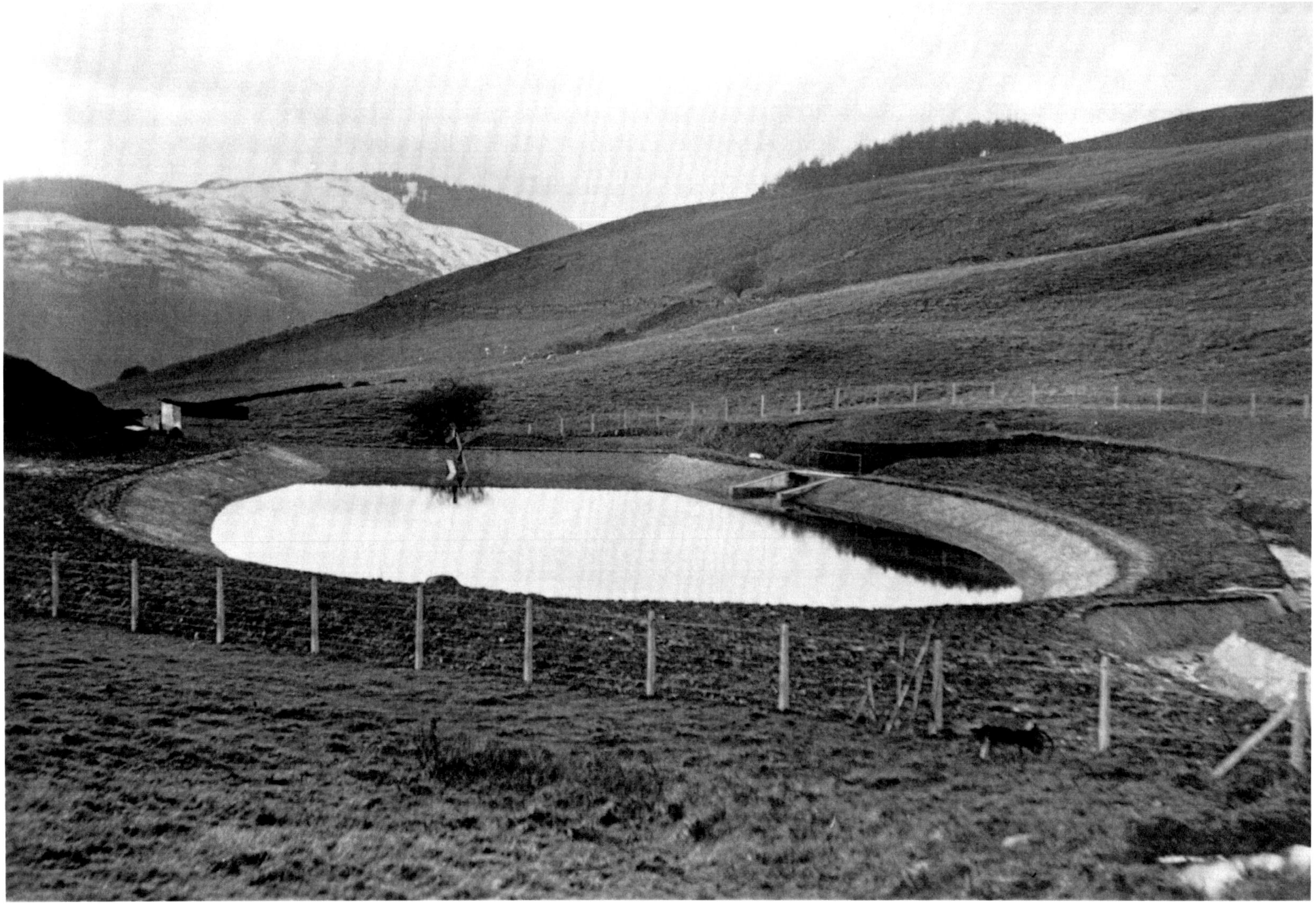

The reservoir was the water supply for the village opened on Barbuie Farm by Colonel and Mrs Walker in the early 1880s.

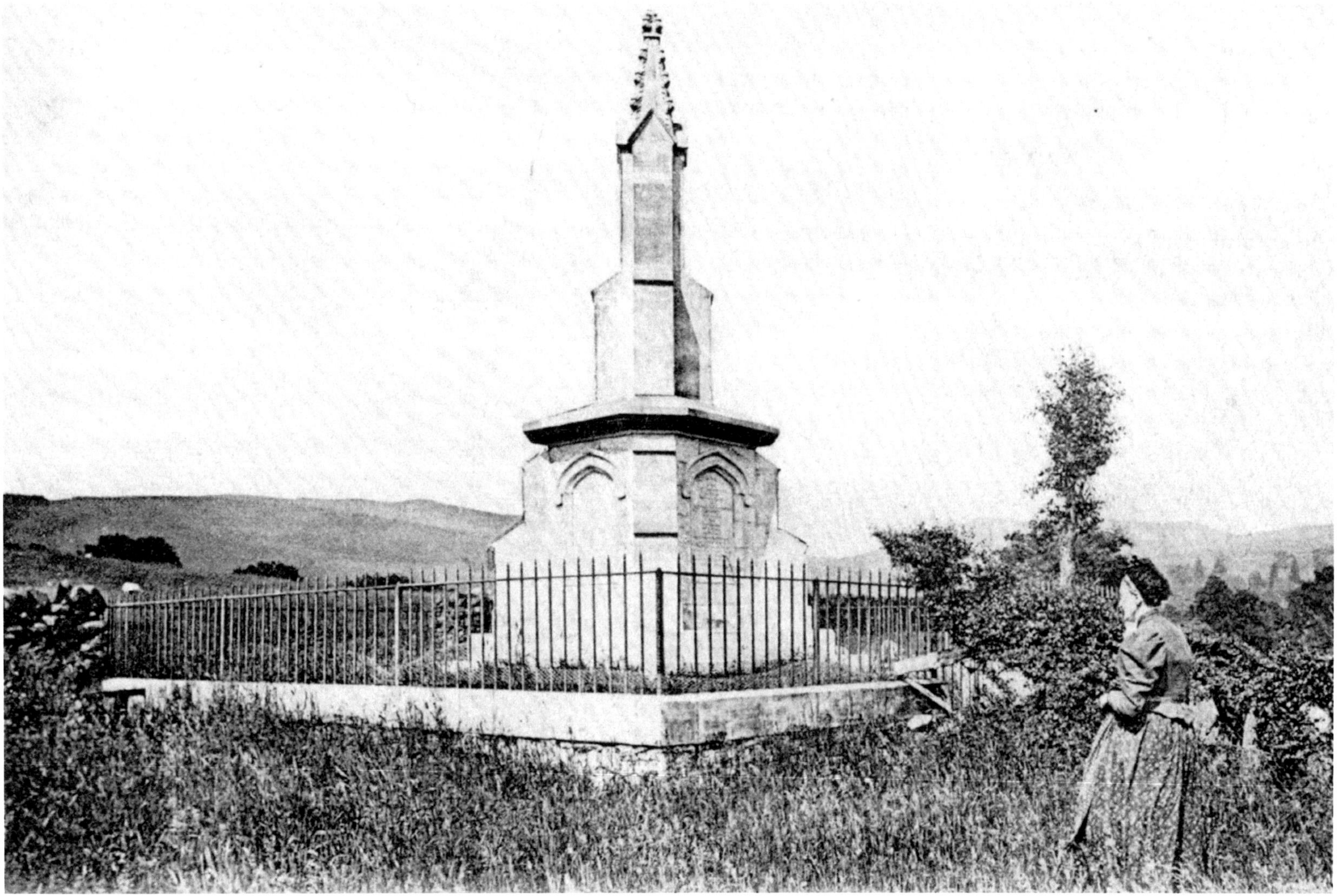

The Renwick Monument around 1905. It is a memorial to the Covenanters and was built in 1828. James Renwick was born in Moniaive in about 1662, the son of a weaver who went to university and then became a Covenanting minister. At the age of 26 he was executed in Edinburgh.

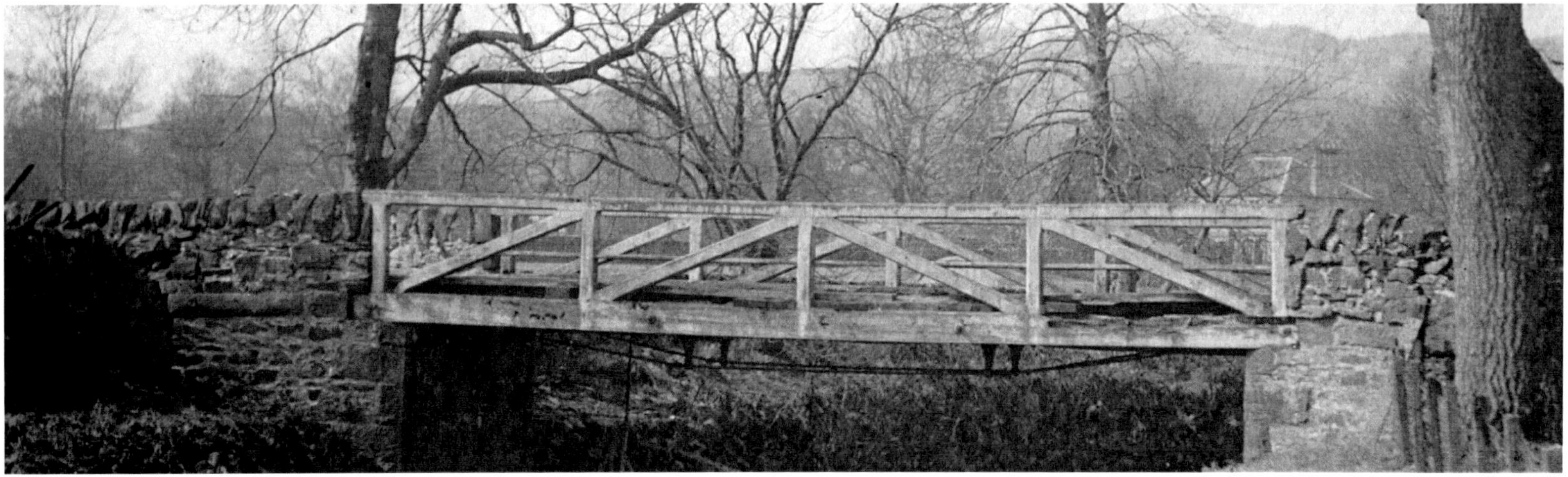

Bardennoch wooden bridge in 1910.

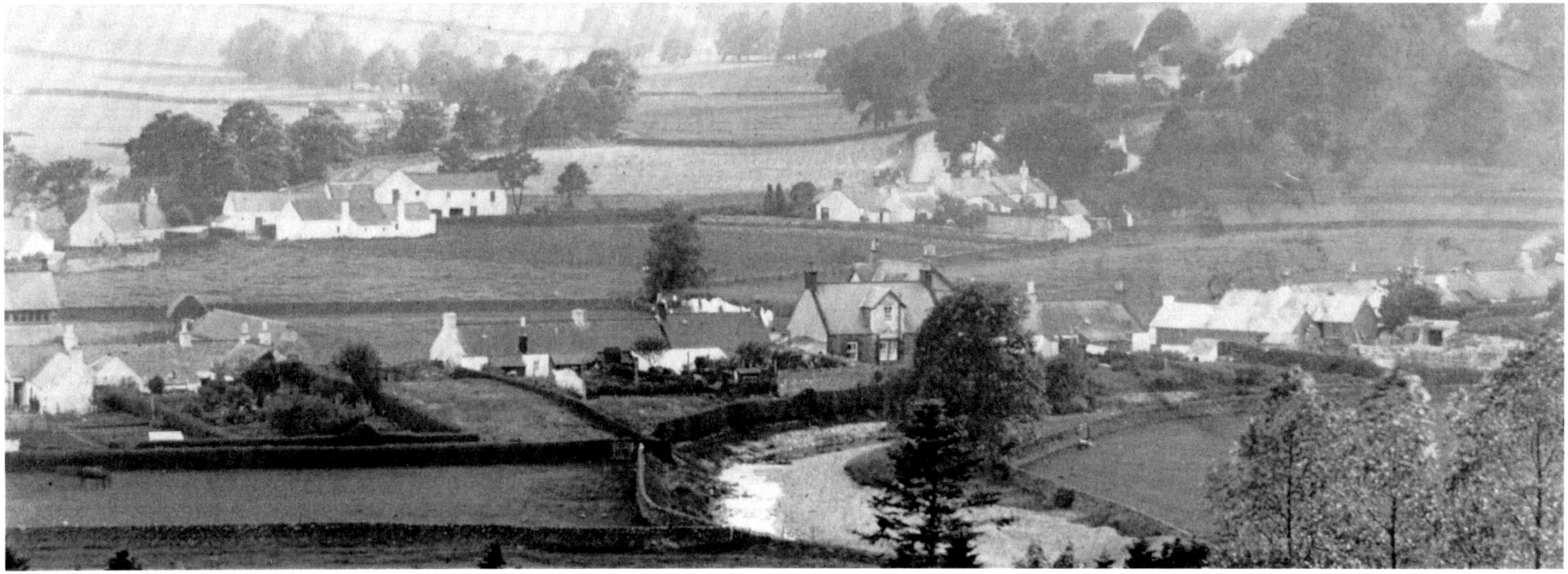

General view of Moniaive in 1910. The Renwick Monument can be seen on the right in the far distance. The corn mill is on the left.

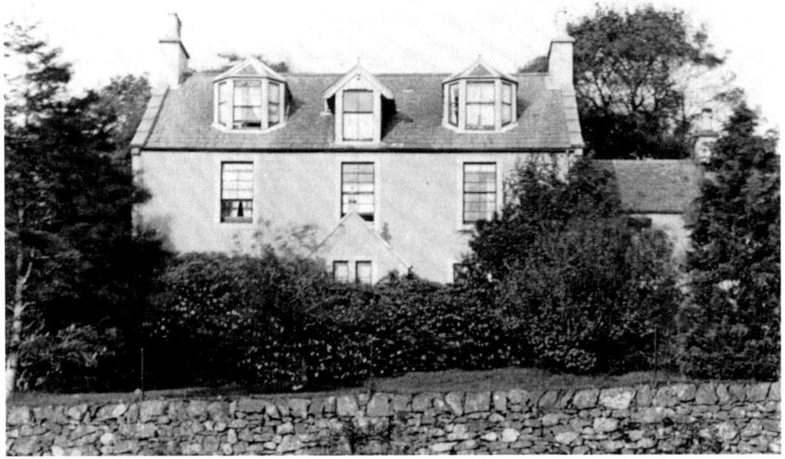

Terreran, seen here in 1912, was owned by Mr William Barber.

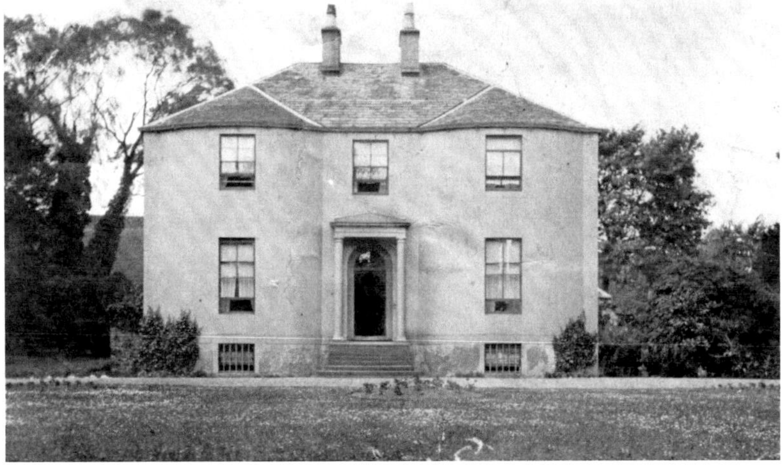

Broomfield Bank House around 1910 when it was owned by Mrs McColl, a widow. Commander Lennox (RN) had this built for his sisters. He is buried in Glencairn Churchyard.

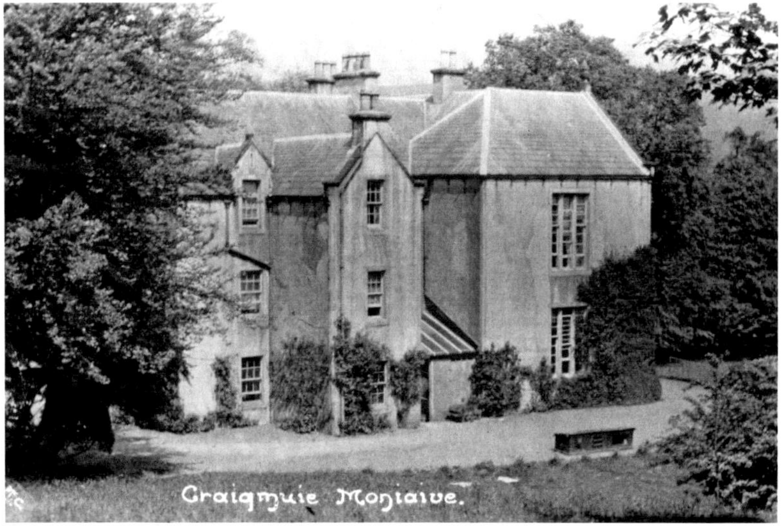


Craigmuie in 1914. This belonged to a land agent called George Gourley.

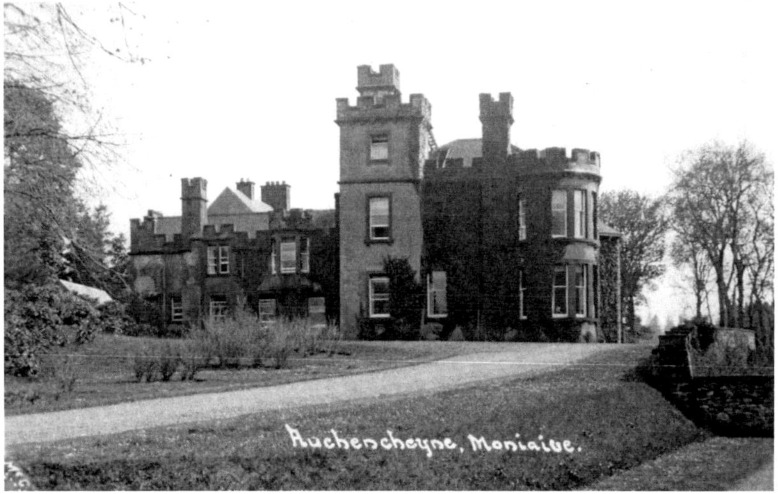


Auchencheyne was built by the Glasgow shipbuilder, Connell and owned by William Kennedy Moffat in 1911.

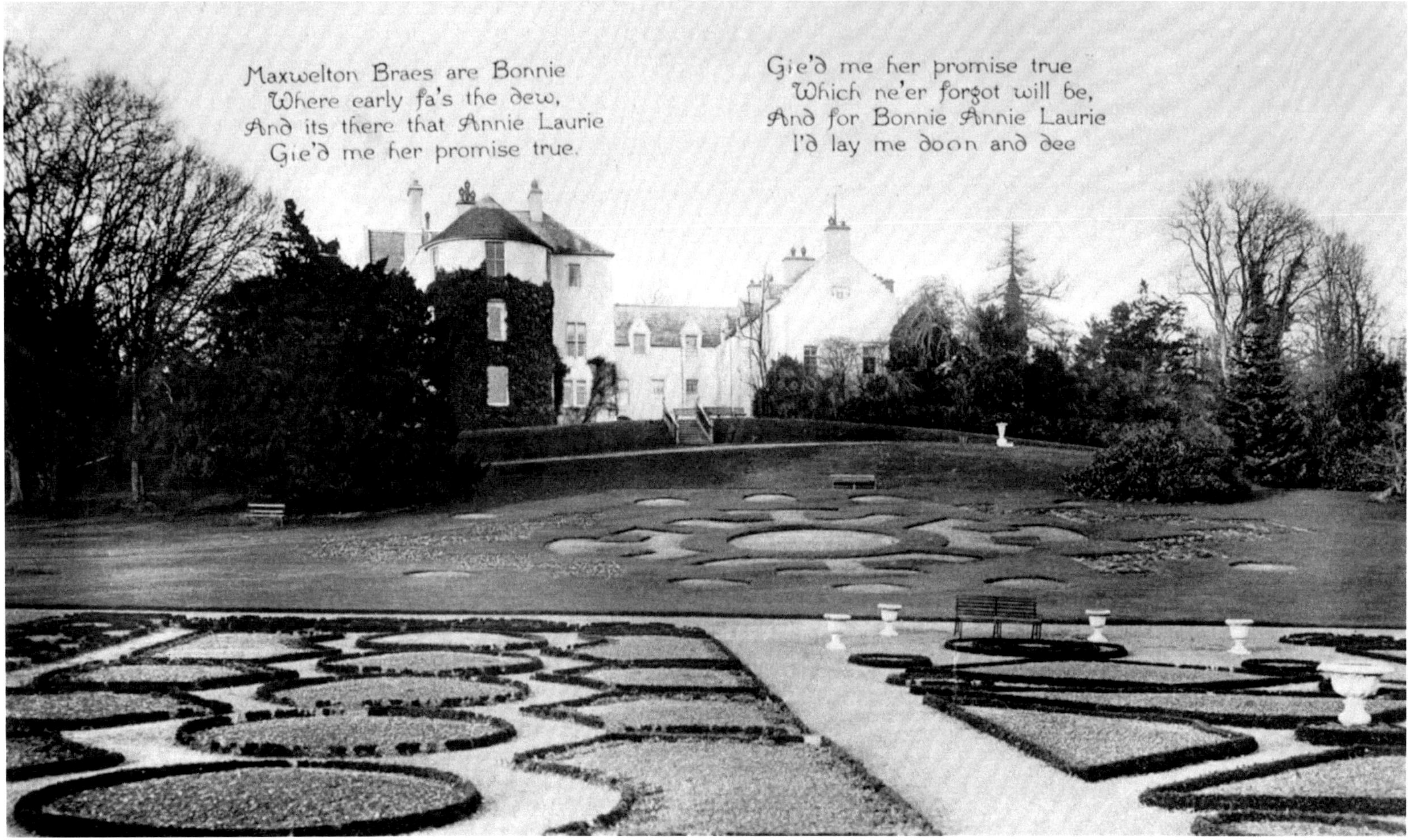


Maxwelton House was the birthplace, in 1682, and childhood home of Annie Laurie about whom the famous song was written. William Douglas of Fingland composed the verses in about 1700 when he was in love with Annie. The romance ended, however, and they went their separate ways. The house occupies the site of the castle of Glencairn destroyed by fire in the 18th century. Annie Laurie was the daughter of Sir Robert Laurie and Jean Riddell. His parents' marriage stone is preserved over the old doorway – JL and AG (John Laurie and Agnes Grierson of Lag). Maxwelton House was occupied by a Norwegian army field battery, under the command of a Major Ringdal in 1941. At that time the Lauries still owned the building and considered them good tenants. Later the Norwegian nursing service was billeted in the house.

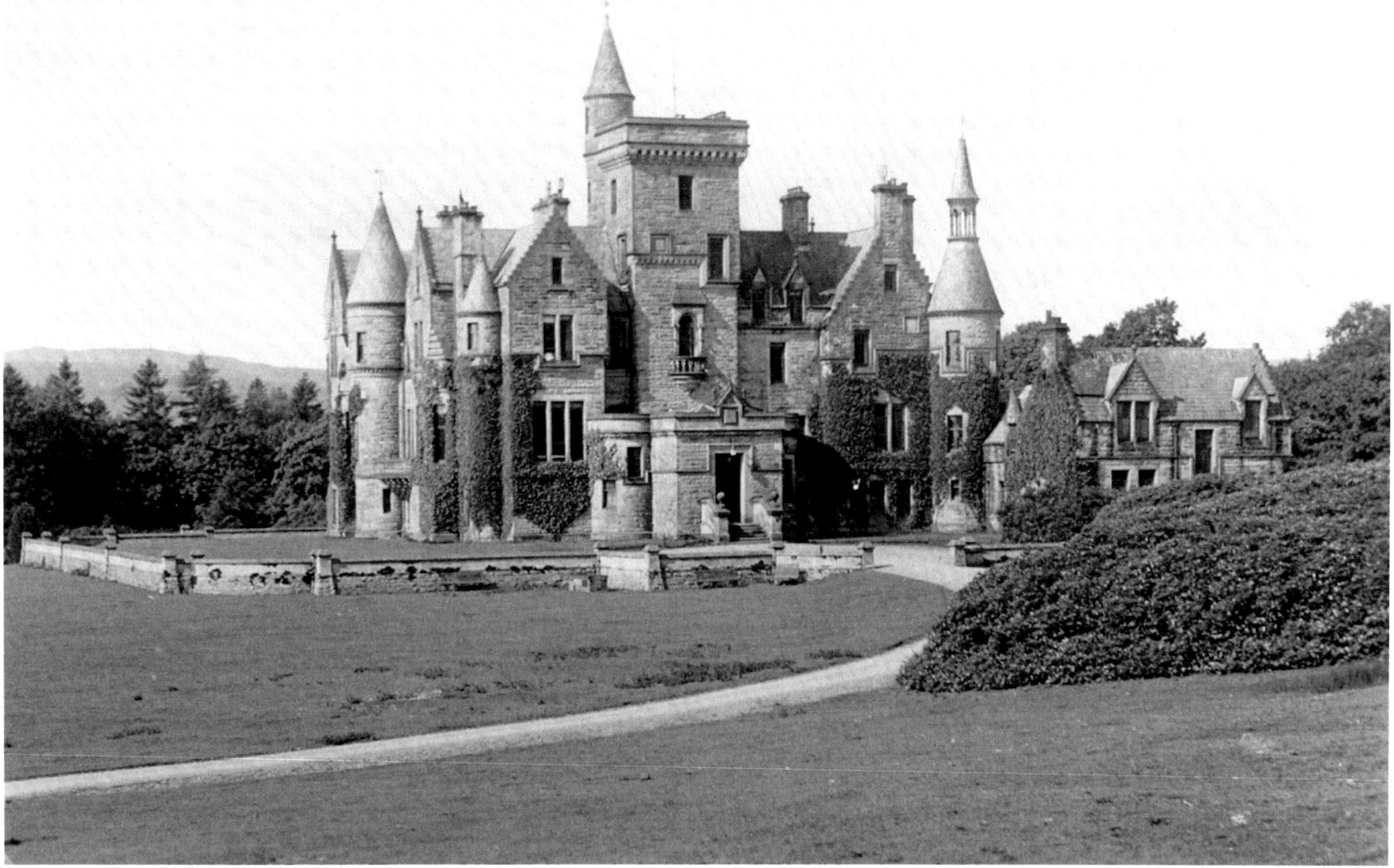

Crawfordton House was built by Colonel George Walker (Conservative MP) in 1865. The architects were Peddie and Kinnear designing in the Scottish baronial style. Boys along with their teacher from Belmont Private School in East Renfrewshire were evacuated here during the Second World War. It continued as a school until the 1990s.

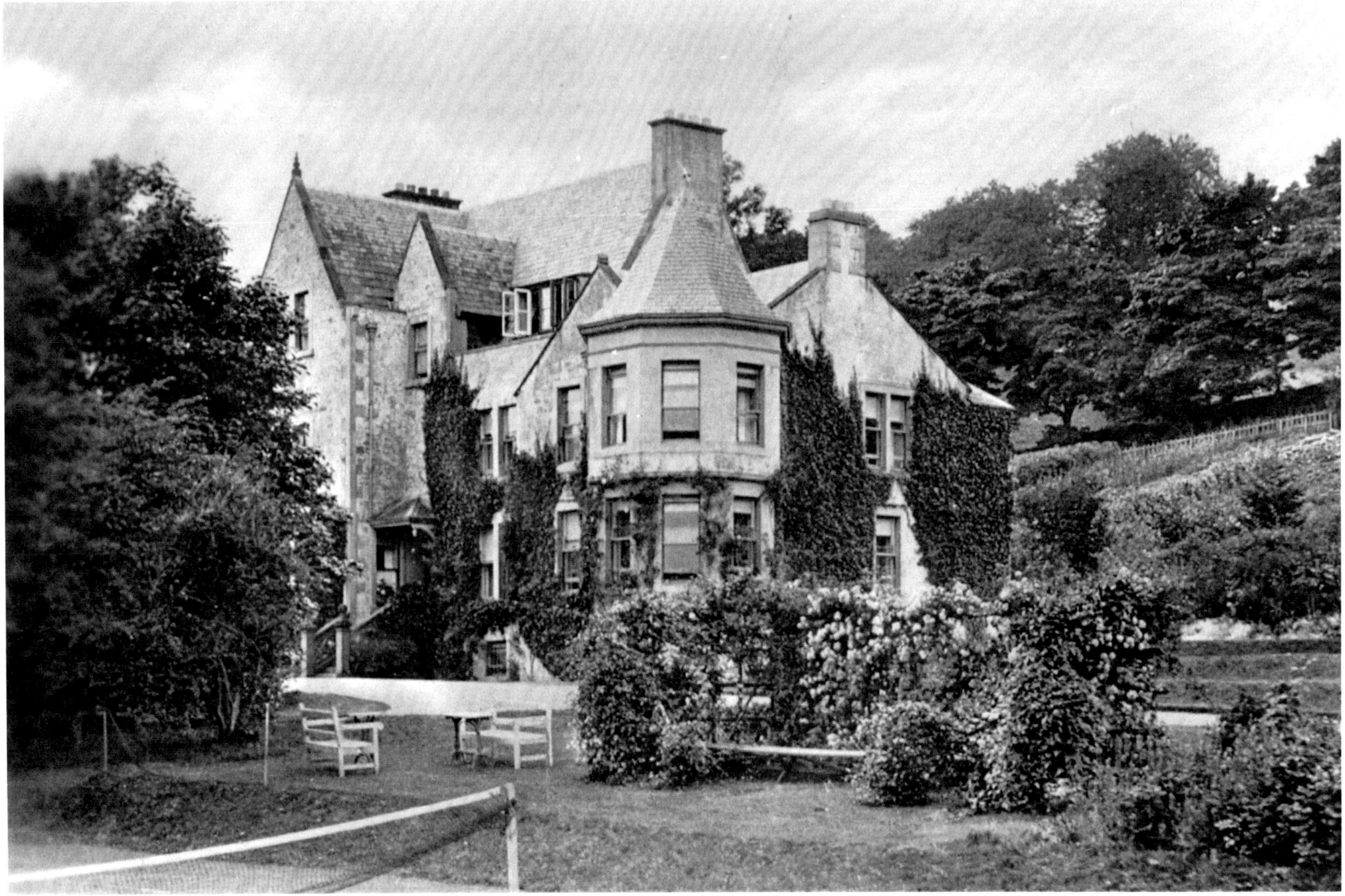

Woodlea, on Dalry Road, around 1922. This house was built by McMillan on the site of a farm called Upper Kirkcudbright. At one time it was a hotel run by Robin McIvor.

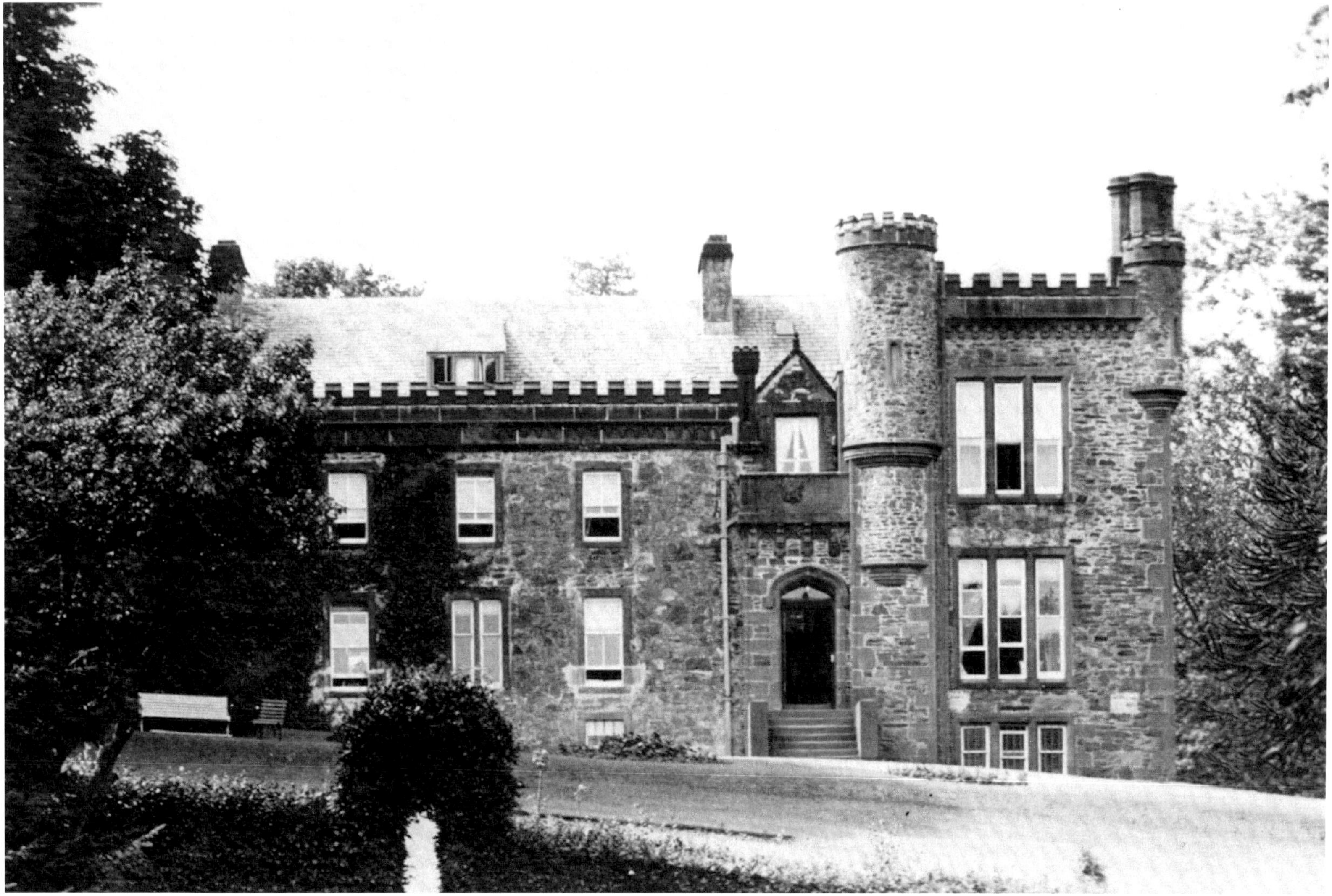

Caitloch was originally a tower house in the 1680s. The McCall family, a branch of the Fergussons, extended it with the addition of battlements, corner turrets and a "Tudor" arch doorway in the 19th century. Nearby are Caitloch Cave and a disused lead mine.

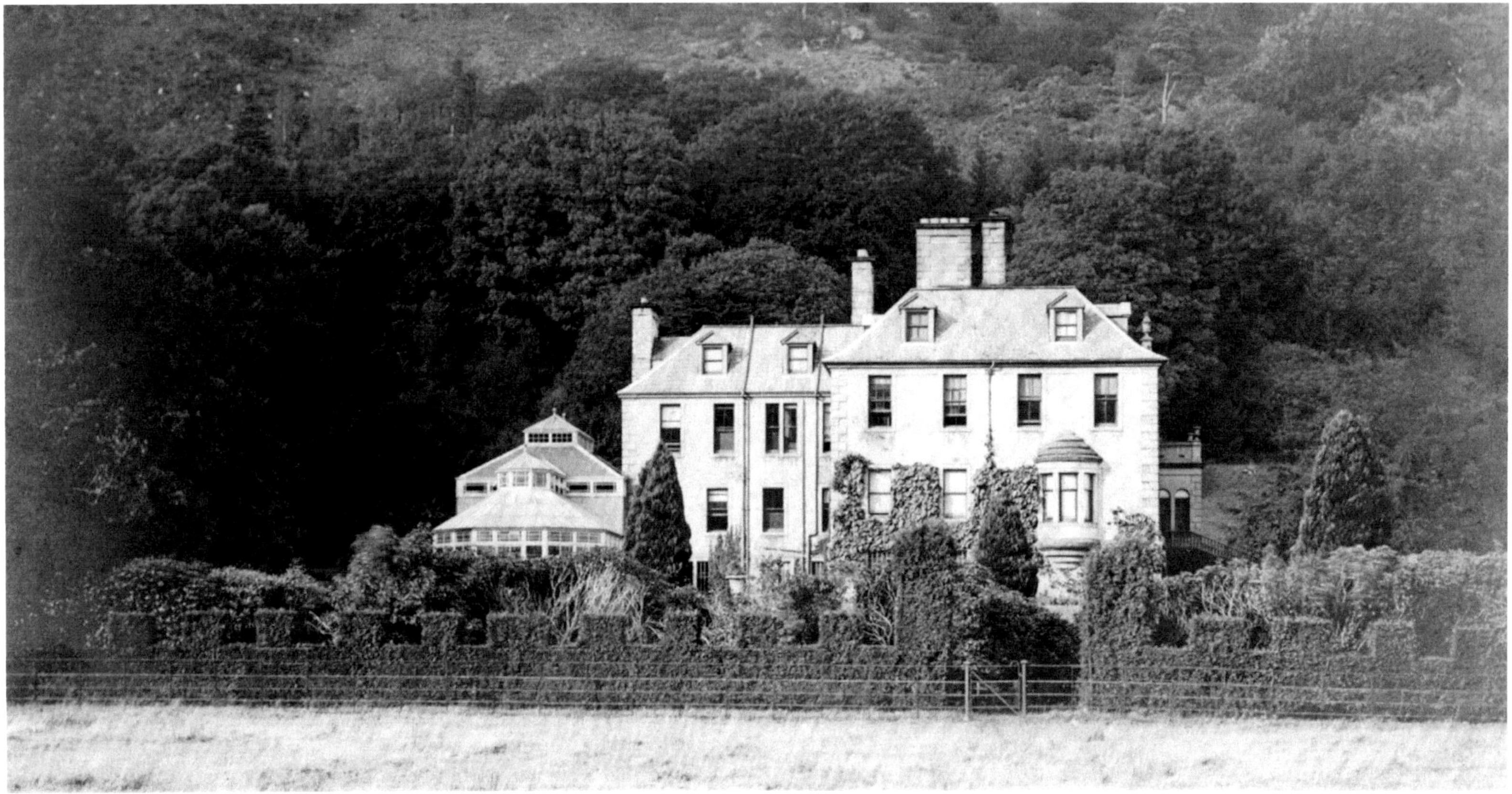

The classical mansion house of Craigdarroch was completed by William Adam in 1729 on the site of a much earlier tower house, the turnpike staircase of which still exists. William's brother, Robert Adam, designed and made the fireplace in the hall. The chapel, built in 1889 by John Starforth, is constructed from oak and stone from the estate and the small stone building in the grounds was where the minister would get changed out of his riding clothes to conduct services in the chapel. The house was the seat of the Fergussons until the 20th century and it was here that Annie Laurie lived for over 50 years in the 18th century once she became the bride of the laird, Alexander Fergusson. Their marriage stone can be seen at the front of the house. Bonnie Prince Charlie spent two nights there in 1745 while the family, who opposed the Jacobites, camped in the hills. In 1940 it became home to a unit of the Norwegian Army. Captain Ingvald Marm's account of his wartime experiences in Dumfriesshire can be found in Dumfries Museum. He stated that Craigdarroch was situated in a "rather desolate and thinly populated area. There were only sheep farms… therefore we had ample opportunity to carry on military exercises… it was a lonely place… the nearest built up area was Moniaive." However Moniaive had a pub and the town soon became a bit livelier! Norwegian naval cooks fed the 150 men. The fare once included a sheep, which had got in the way of the firing line!

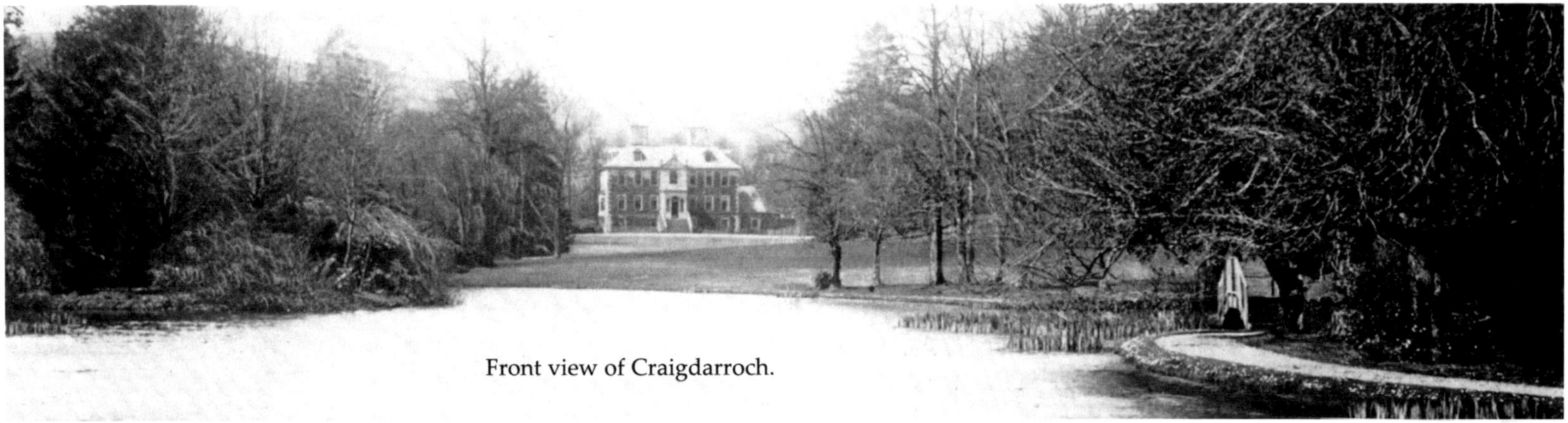

Front view of Craigdarroch.

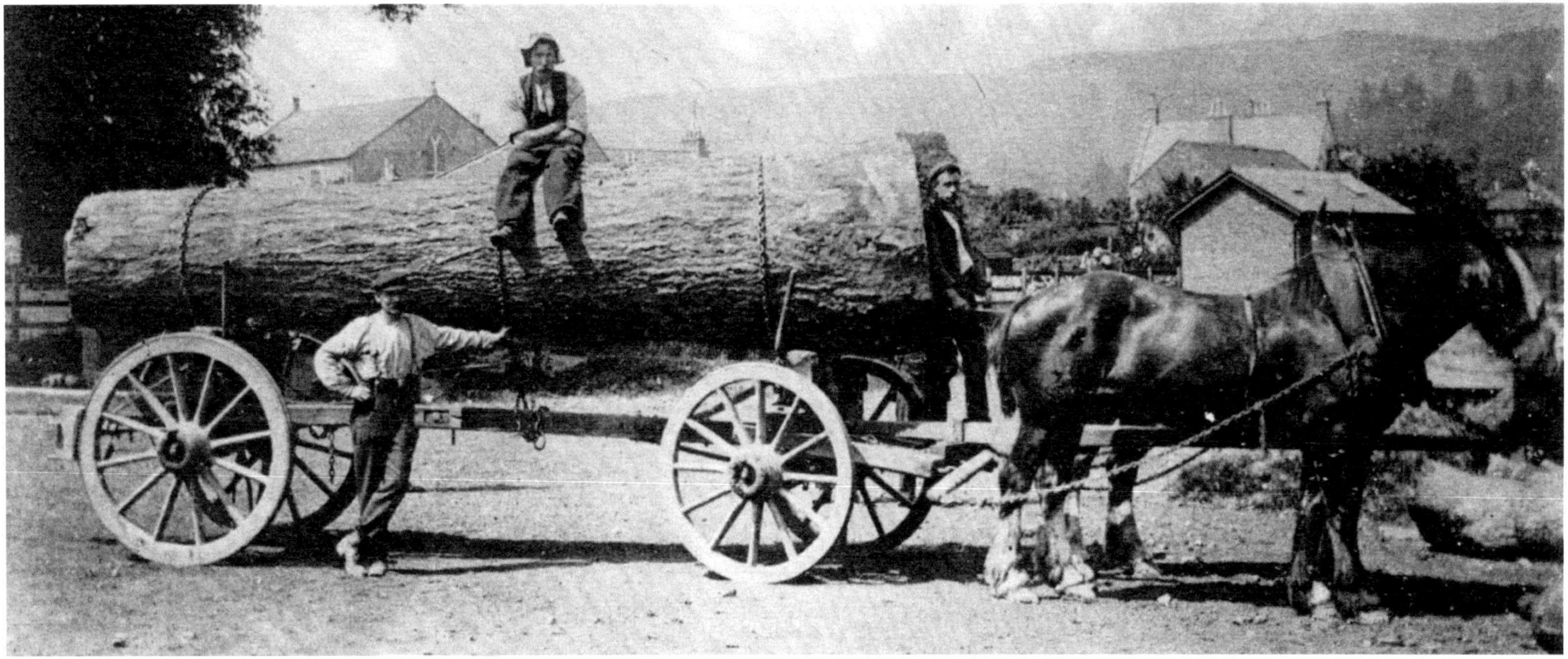

This Edwardian photograph shows one of the larch trees from the Craigdarroch estate. In the 19th and early 20th century there was a sawmill.

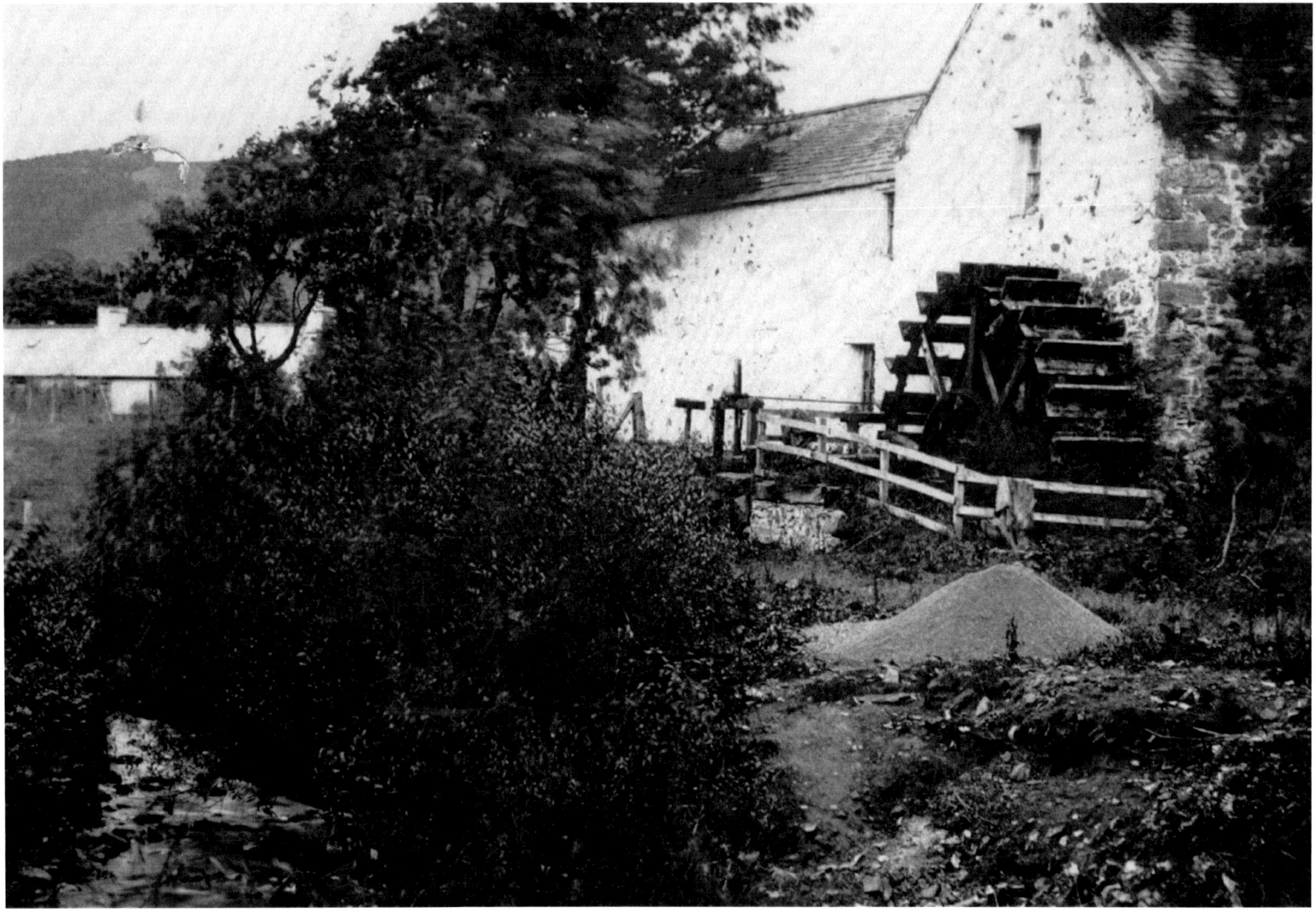

The mill and the water wheel. 1911.

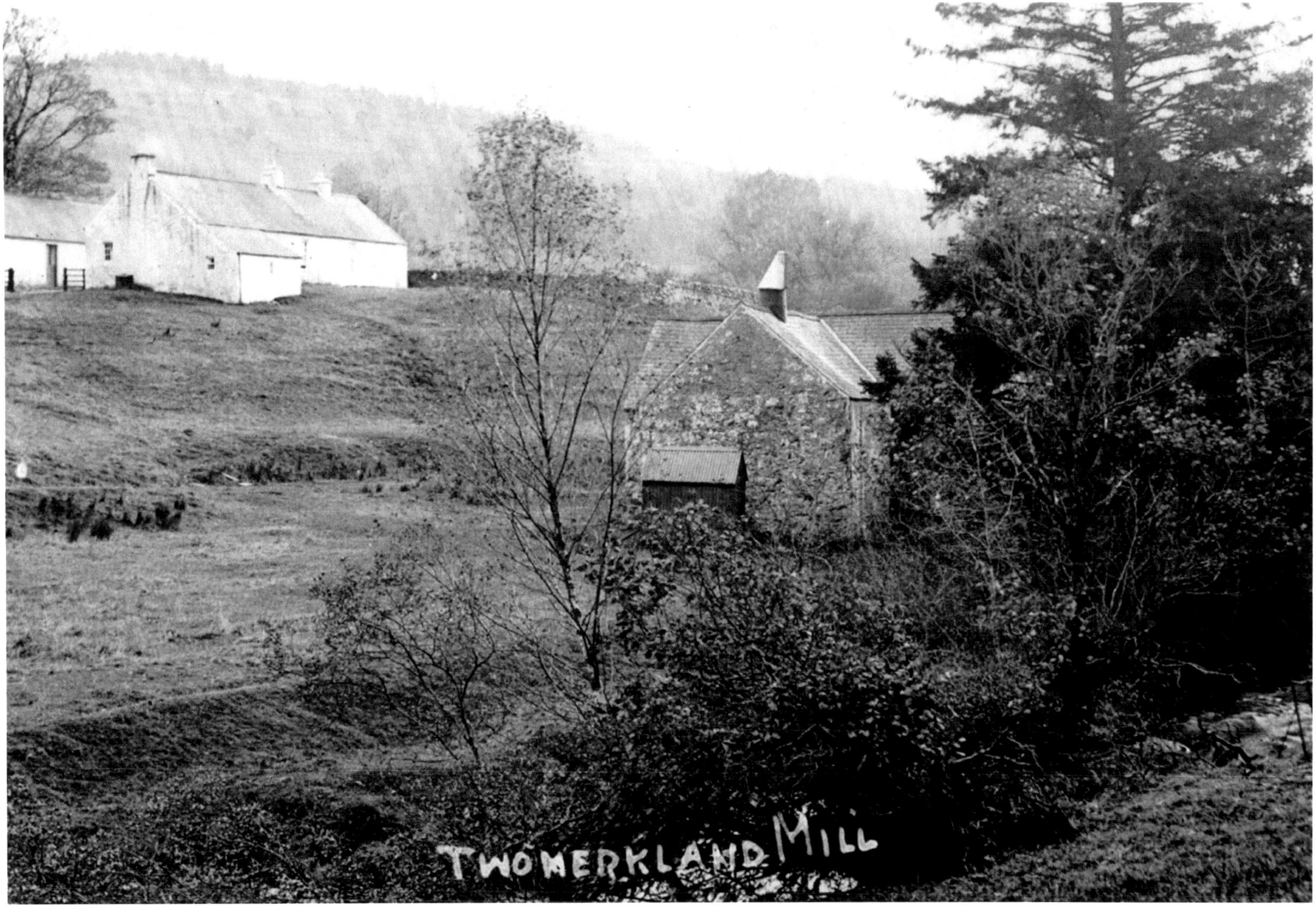


Two Merkland Farm, situated on the road to Dalry, with the miller's house and byre on the left.

# Dunscore

A settlement probably existed here around 1500 BC according to archaeological evidence of cairns and hut circles. The existence of crannogs in Carse Loch near Friars' Carse and a Celtic hillfort at Springfieldhill further add to its antiquity and Roman forts have been found at Carzield, Dalswinton and Bamburgh Hill. Dun being the word for fort possibly gave the parish its name although Dunscore also means the hill with the steep rock. Monks from a 6th century monastery at nearby Holywood owned most of the land in the Cairn Valley and were possibly the founders of the village of Cottack (for cottars or small holders) which was then renamed Dunscore in the 19th century. The parish is situated in Nithsdale and measures about 11 miles from east to west and lies about nine miles from Dumfries. The scenery contains rough heathery hillsides as well as flat fertile countryside. Bogrie Hill, at a height of 1416 feet, is the highest point and the Cairn River flows through the parish from nearby Moniaive down to the Nith at Lincluden. There are several large country houses throughout the parish as well as the towers of Lag, Bogrie and Sundaywell.

Records show that there were schools in the parish by 1738 and, by 1748, the schoolmaster was receiving an income of £11 annually. After the 1872 Education Act, which made school compulsory from ages 5 to 13, there were three schools in the parish. One was a small school at Glenesslin, which remained until the mid 20th century, one at Burnhead and one in Dunscore village, which later became a reading room and village hall. A newer school was built on the outskirts of the village in the 1900s, but closed in 1963. A modern school now sits in the former school's playground.

At the far end of the valley Robert Burns wrote many of his most famous works: *Tam o' Shanter*, *Auld Lang Syne* and *Ae Fond Kiss* whilst farming Ellisland from 1788 until 1791. From there he often walked along the banks of the Nith to visit his friend, Robert Riddell, at nearby Friars' Carse.

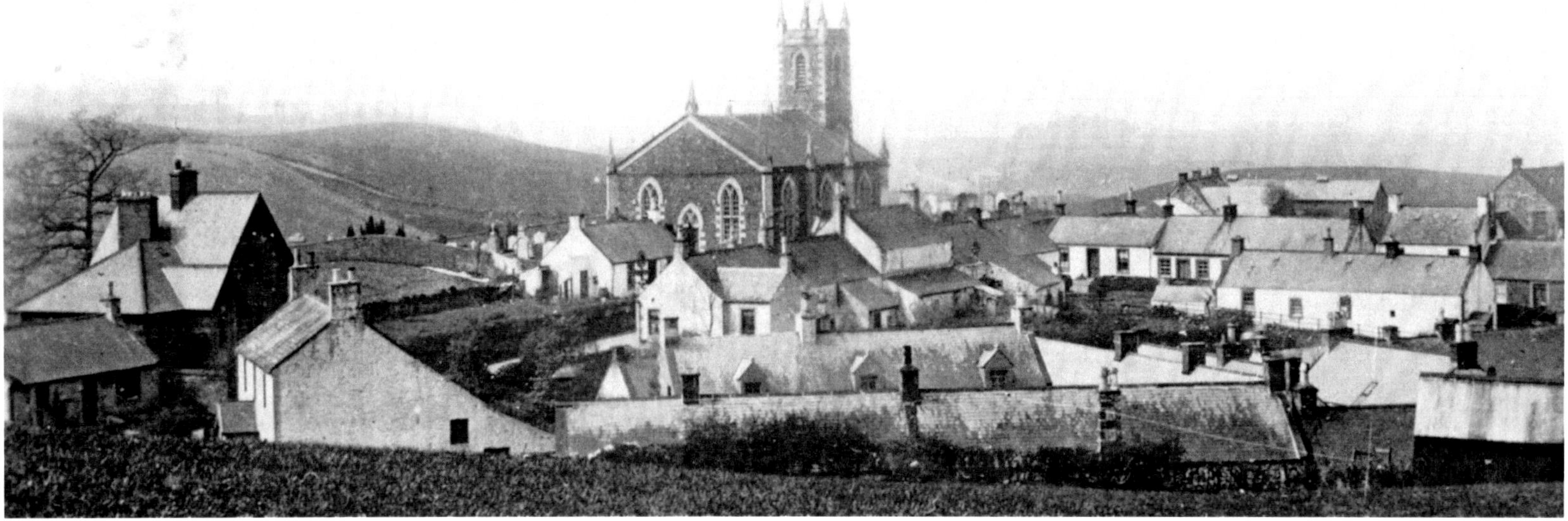

Dunscore Village in about 1919. Amongst the shops were grocers, butchers, bootmakers, and tailors. The schoolmaster in 1911 was Mr D Gold; the constable was R McDonald and Miller Irving was the proprietor of the King's Arms Hotel. The parish church can be seen in the centre of the village.

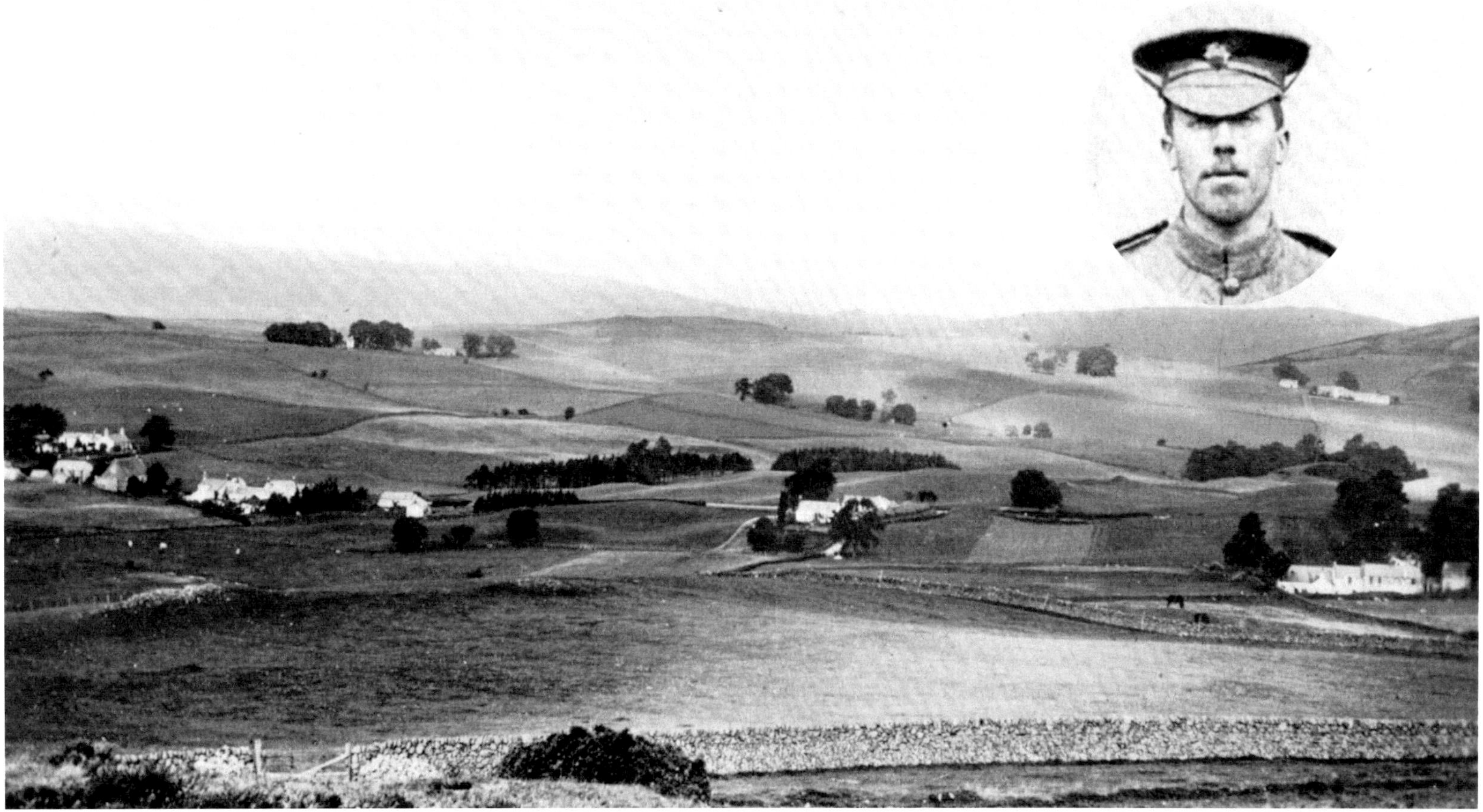

View from Cats Gate, Dunscore district.

*Inset*: Private Thomas Rae, Dunscore, first battalion of Scots Guards. Private Rae had boarded in Dunscore and is on the church's Roll of Honour, but he was born in Lochmaben in the Annandale Valley. He is commemorated on the Dunscore War Memorial as well as at Loos Cemetery in France. At only 21 he died on 27th September 1915. The Battle of Loos was where many Scots lost their lives and has been called a second Flodden. Rudyard Kipling's son and the brother of the old Queen Mother were amongst the fallen. Although he doesn't seem to have been related there is another Private Rae commemorated on the Dunscore memorial as well as on a family gravestone in the old churchyard. Robert Rae was in the Machine Gun Corps and is commemorated at Nine Elms British cemetery, Belgium. He died aged 25 on 4th March 1918.

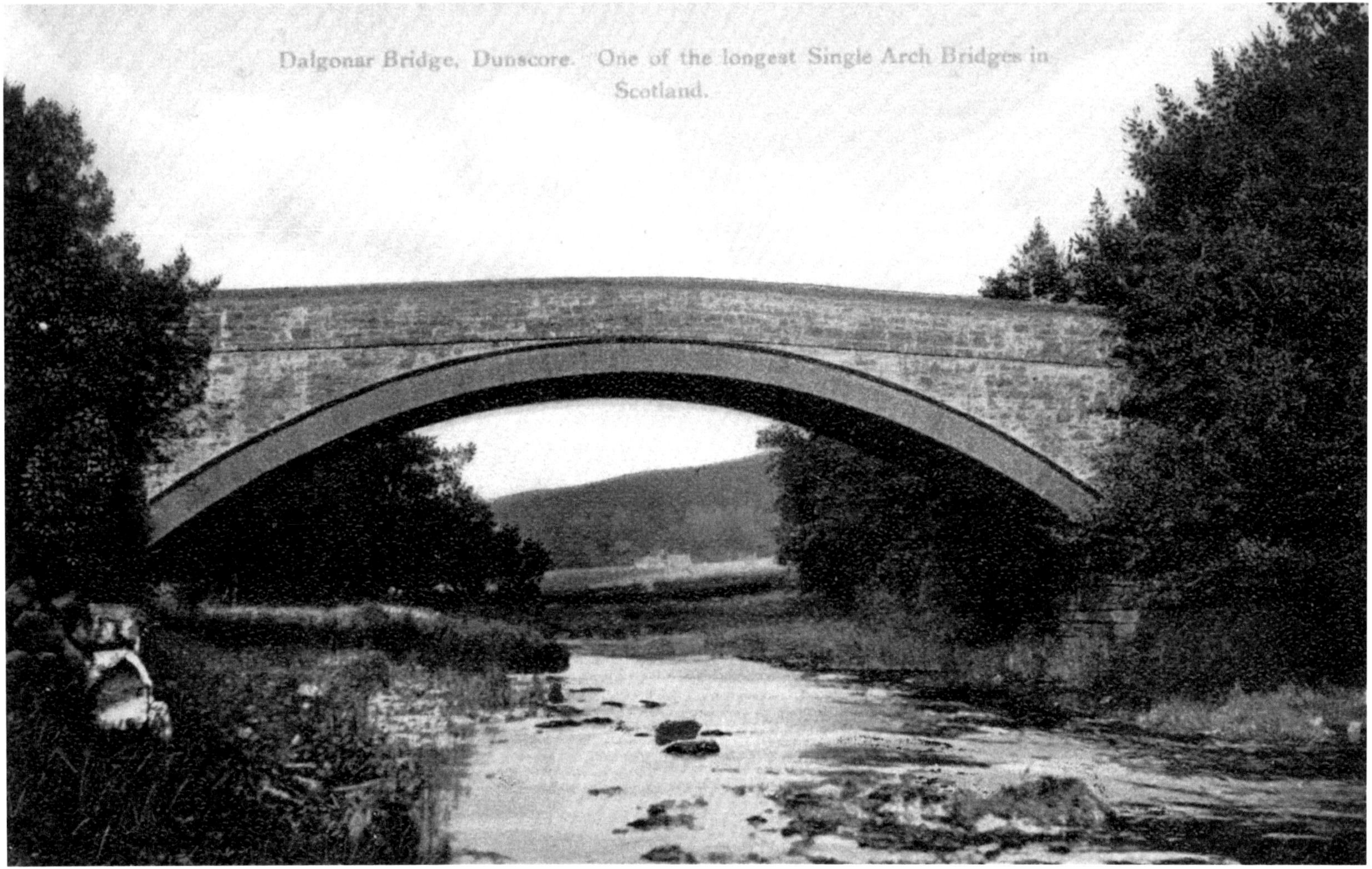


Dalgonar Bridge, a half mile south west of Dunscore on the Dunscore – Corsock Road, over the River Cairn. This is one of the longest single arch bridges in Scotland (spans 75 feet). In 1729 the heritors petitioned for a new bridge to replace the old timber one "now in ruinous condition". John Frew was paid, in 1736, £1920 Scots, but it was in need of repair in 1759 when William Douglas was paid £20 and again in 1805 John Gracie was paid £31. 12/- (three years earlier £32 had been granted for these repairs!) There used to be a grain-threshing mill near to this bridge, which remained until the 20th century.

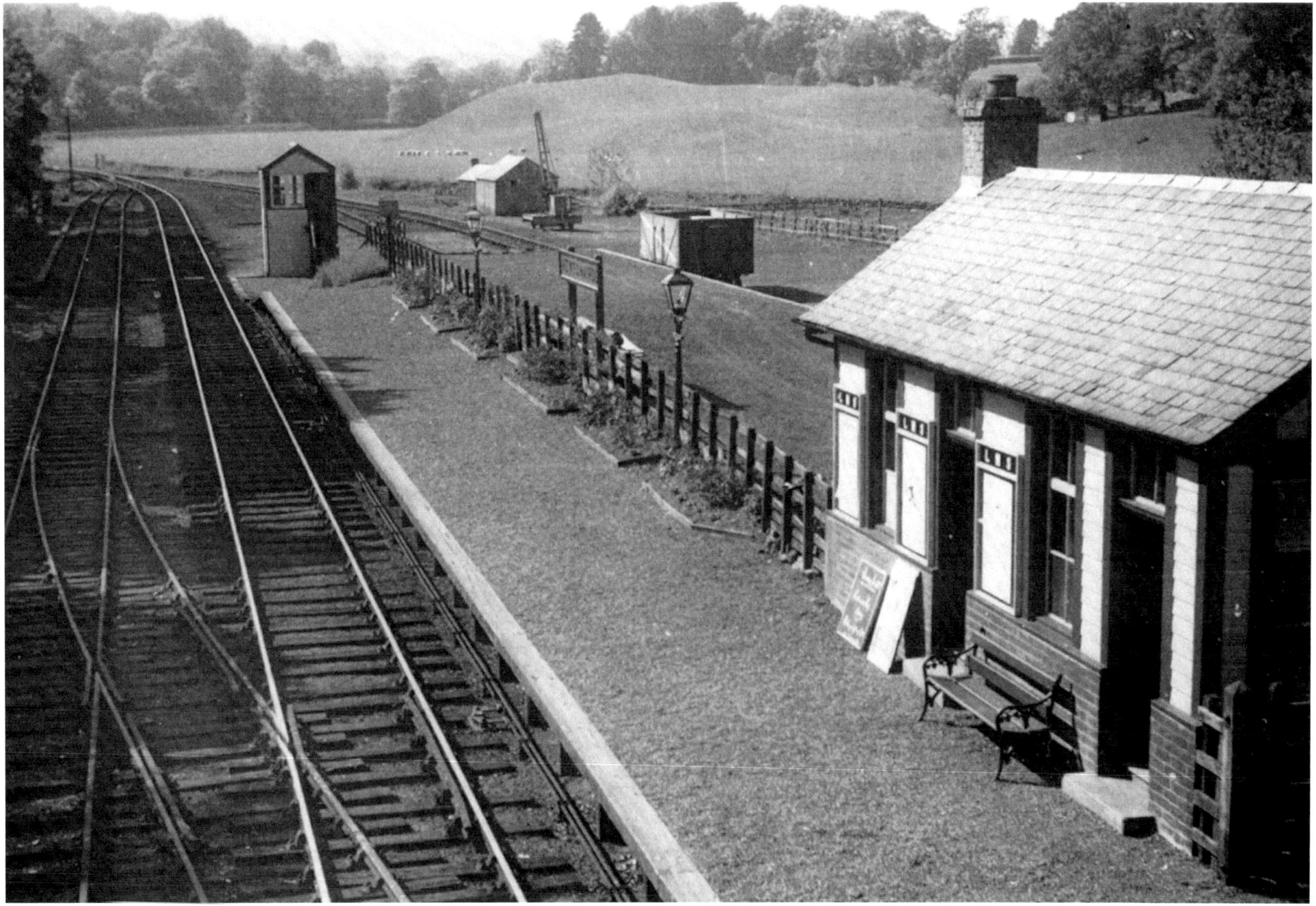

Newtonairds Station had a goods yard and station office.

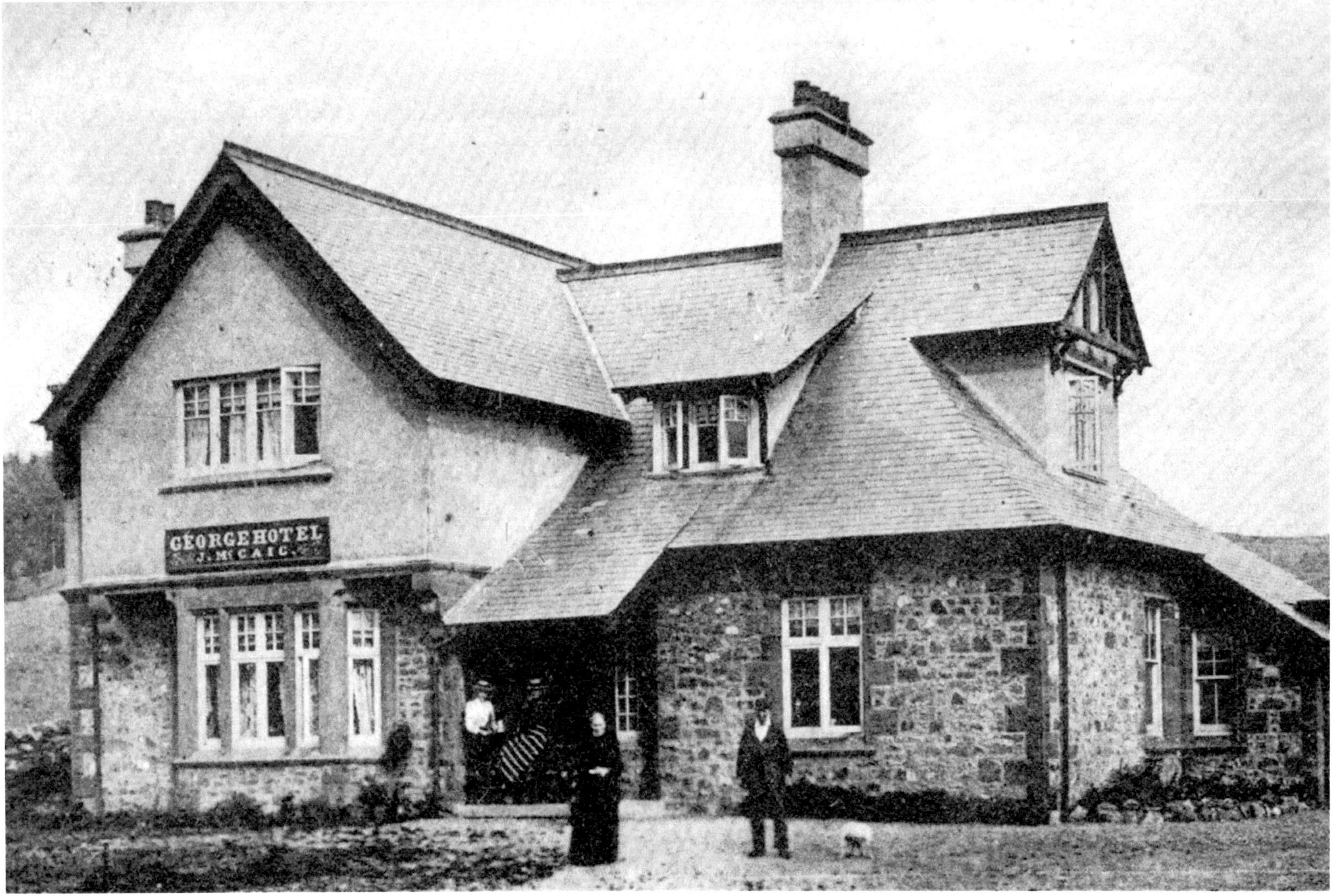


This building with the unusual roof housed the George Hotel in Dunscore. The postcard was used in 1904 when J McCaig ran the hotel. In 1911 Michael Aitken was the proprietor.

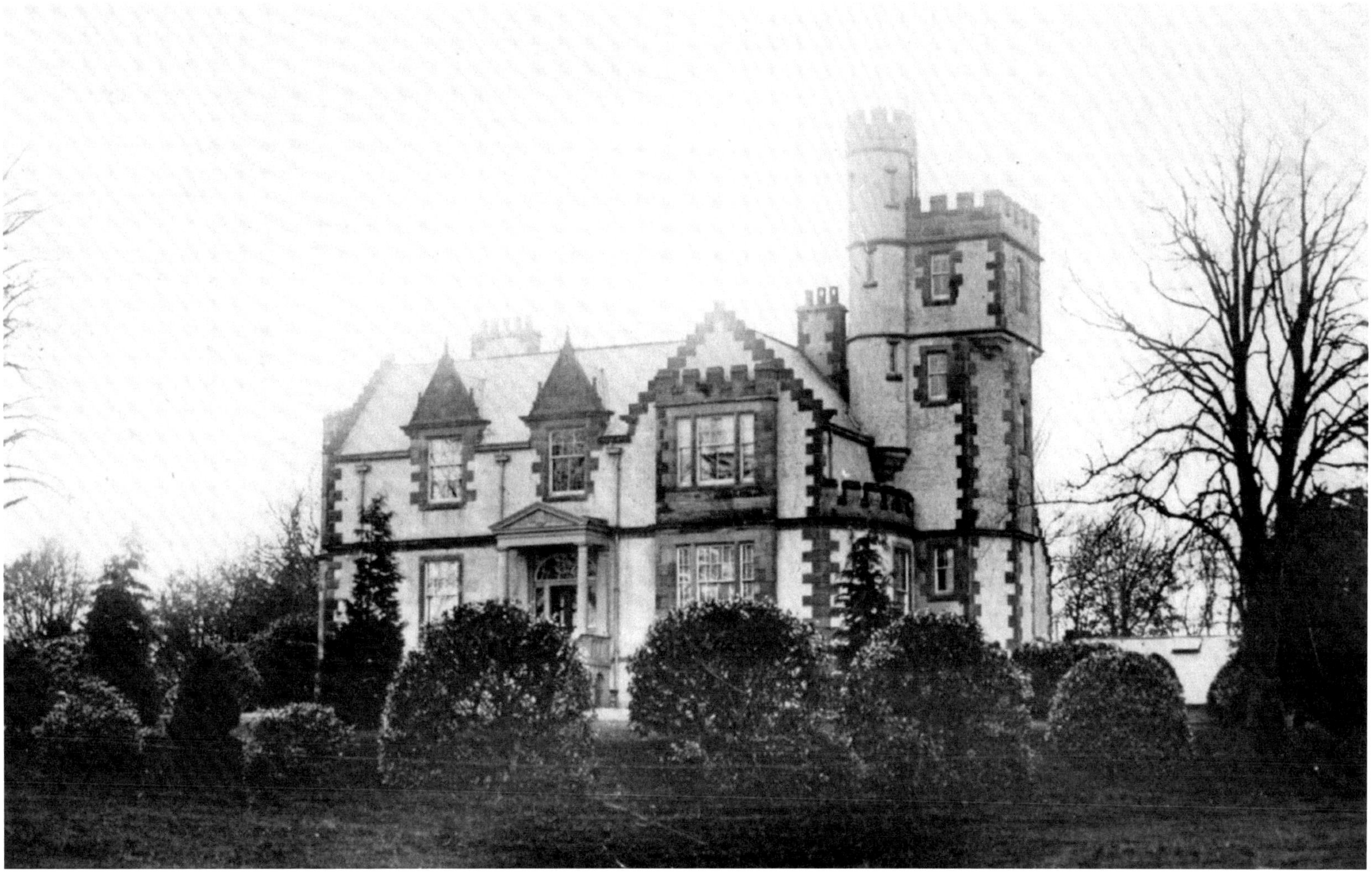

Allanton, Dunscore 1920 This Georgian laird's house was remodelled around 1870 by the Whighams family who owned coal mines in Sanquhar. In the early 1900s the house was burnt down, but then rebuilt by the Symington family. It later became home to the Verona Fathers, an Italian mission, who ran it in the 1960s as a boys' home. It then underwent various guises, but now is the centre for the World Peace Prayer Society as well as a venue for workshops and conferences.

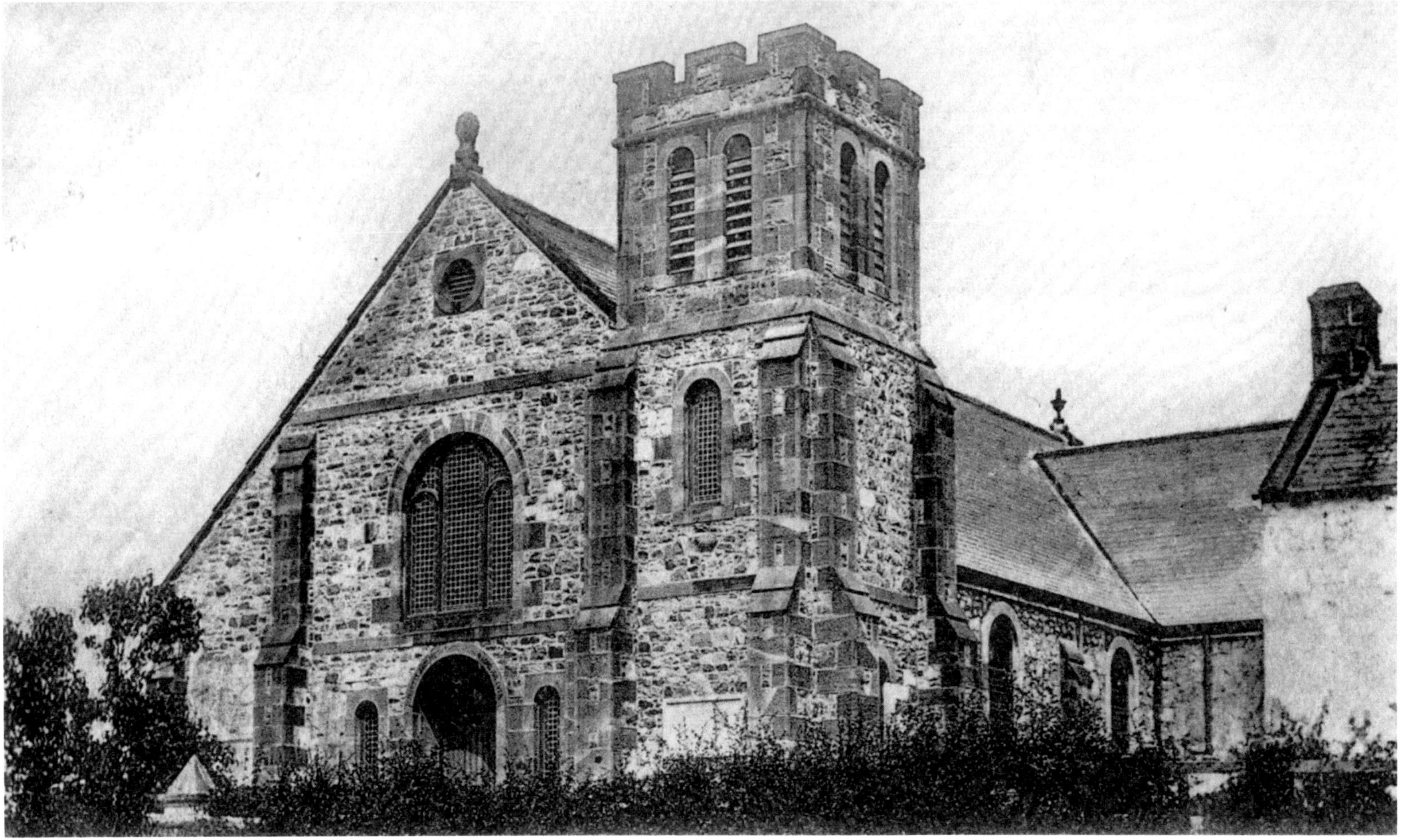

Dunscore East United Free Church around 1904. The church was designed by James Gillison in 1843 and rebuilt in 1899. This church was finally abandoned as a place of worship in 1994. A stone tablet is built into the church wall with the following inscription: - " By voluntary contributions aided by central Fund, erected this place of worship in connexion with the Free Church of Scotland when for conscience sake because they would no surrender to the Civil Power the Spiritual Independence of Christ's Church and the liberties of his people. Nearly 500 ministers gave up their Livings and left the Establishment. MDCCCXL111 Robert Bryden, Minister. At the time of the Great Disruption Free Churches were created throughout Scotland as a result of the break from the Established Church.

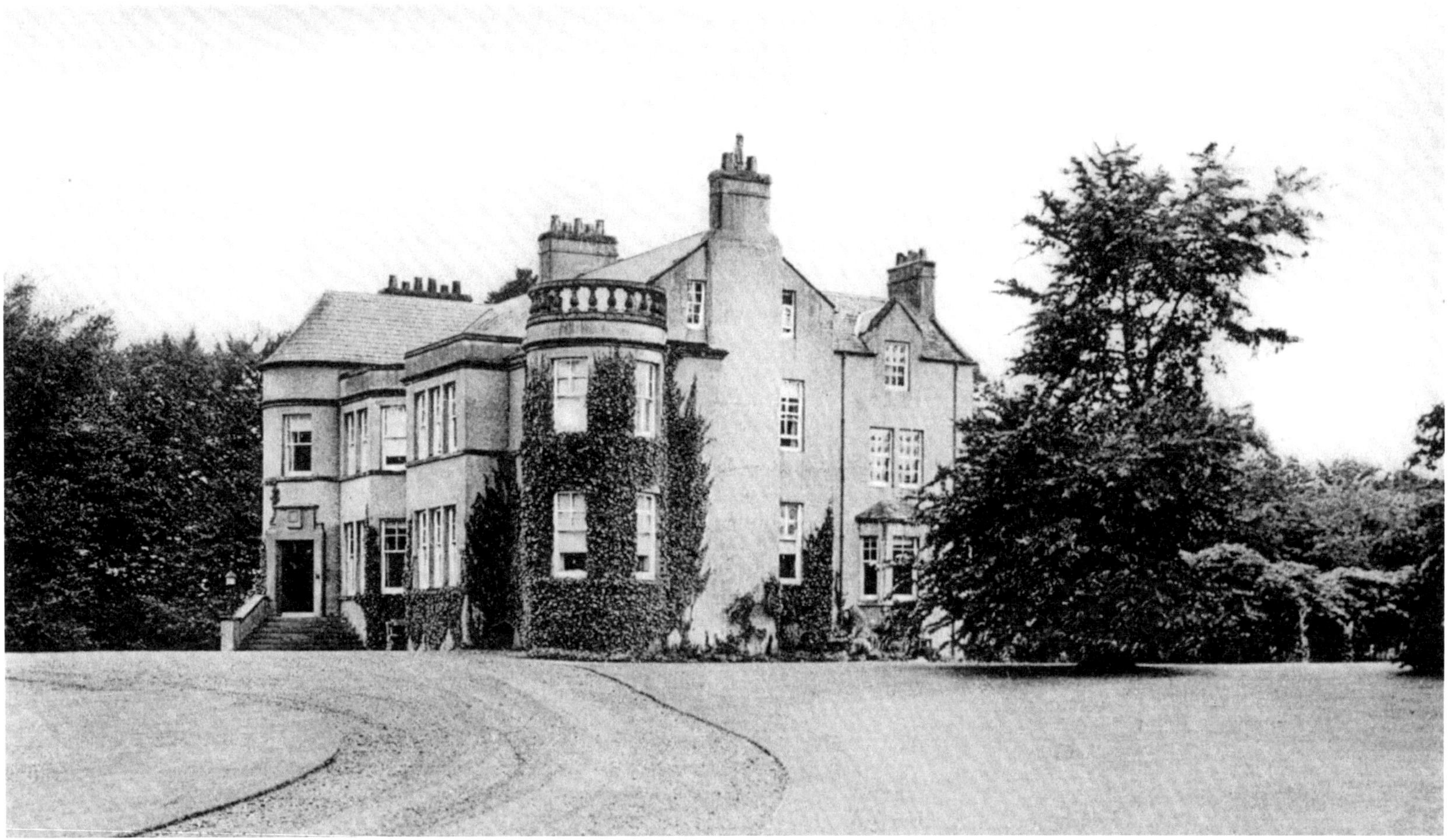

Dalgonar House in 1930. This house dates back to the beginning of the 17th century although the lands of Dalgonar are mentioned in the 13th century belonging to Melrose Abbey. It was to become the ancestral home of the Griersons who modified and extended the house in the 1770s. James Grierson of Dalgonar was famous as a supporter of conventicles – the outlawed outdoor services of the Covenanters – and helped to arrange the famous Communion service attended by 3,000 folk at Skeoch Hill in 1678. Sir Robert Grierson of Lag Tower, however, was associated with John Graham of Claverhouse who hunted down the Covenanters. Nine Covenanters from Moniaive were sentenced to banishment in 1679, but their ship was wrecked off Orkney and five were drowned. The grounds at Dalgonar contain a group of Wellingtonia trees reputedly planted to commemorate the Duke of Wellington. Seedlings of this species of soft bark tree had been discovered in California by William Lobb, brought to Britain in 1853 and named after the recently deceased duke.

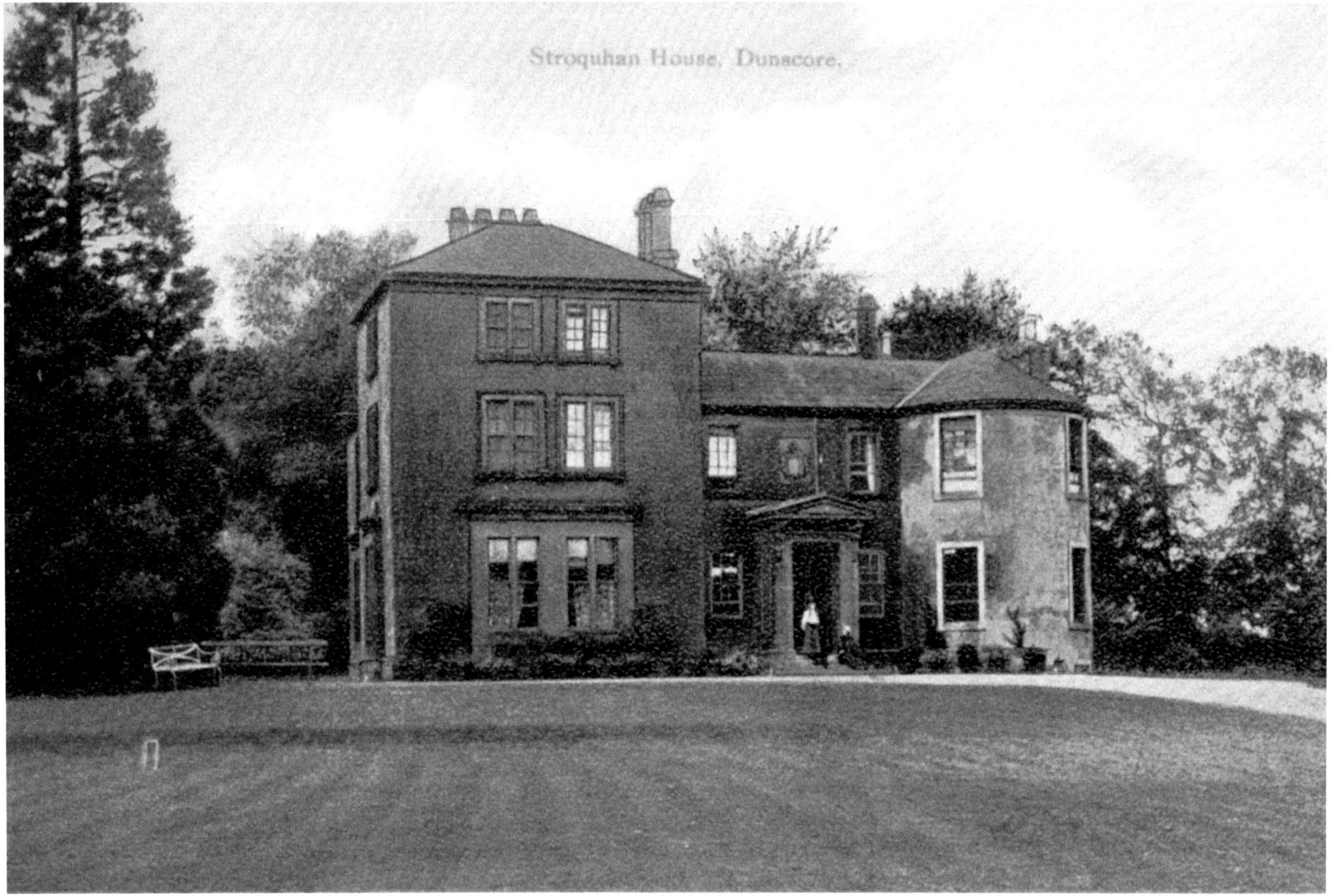


Stroquhan House in 1905. This laird's house was built from red sandstone in the 18th century, but has a Tudor style gate lodge built in 1845. It belonged to the Johnston family and in 1911 it was the home of William Bow. Note the croquet lawn in front of the house.

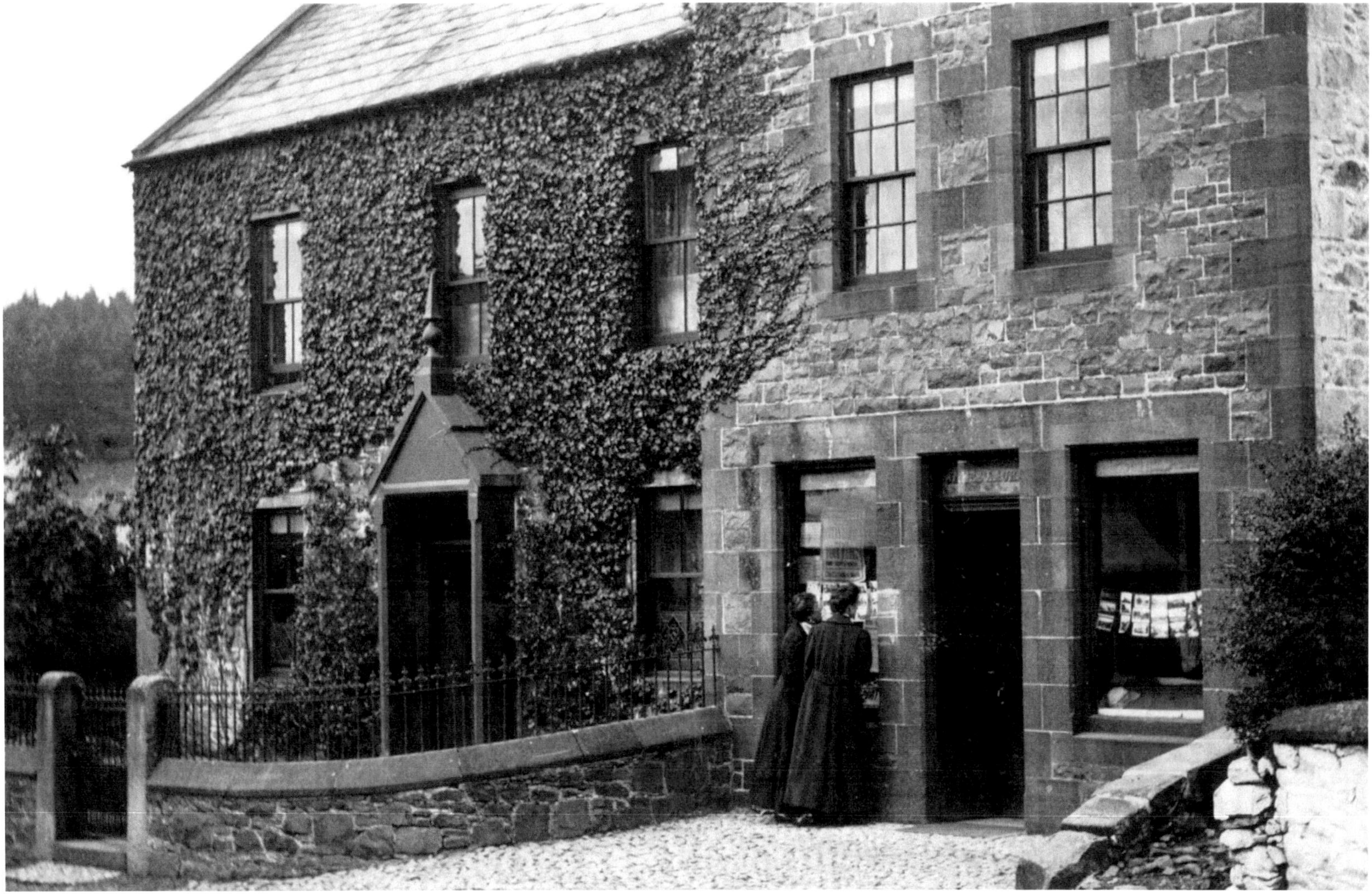

This was the old post office in Dunscore run by Mrs Waugh in 1912. Postcards are displayed in its window. They were a cheap and very popular way folk kept in touch – not solely as holiday mementoes. For example, arrangements to meet at railway stations could be made at the last moment due to the reliability of both the train and postal services.

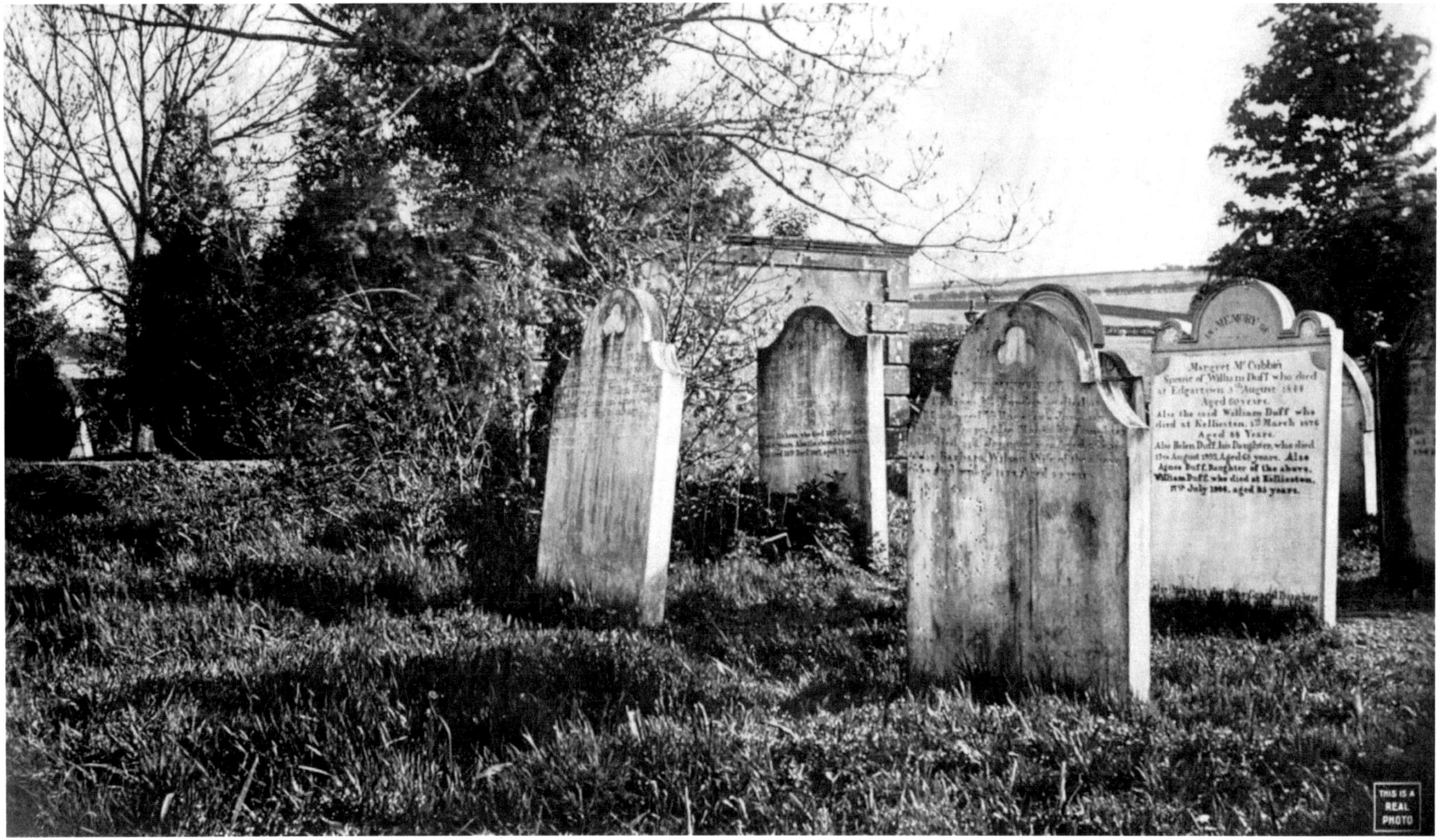


Dunscore Old Churchyard on Coldside Road on the outskirts of the village. In some documents, Old Dunscore is referred to as Portrak. This is the burial place of Robert Riddell (1757-1794) of Friars' Carse and an old friend of Robert Burns. Captain Riddell had married an Elizabeth Kennedy after whom Burns named his daughter. It was at Friars' Carse after a drinking contest, that the two men had a falling out concerning Mrs Riddell. However, later on hearing of his death, Burns wrote *Sonnet on the Death of Robert Riddell*. The churchyard also contains a monument to Sir Robert Grierson of Lag (1650-1736), the persecutor of Covenanters and reputedly responsible for the drowning of Margaret McLachlan and Margaret Wilson, the Wigtown Bay martyrs. The stone for the monument was removed from Lag Tower, the seat of the Griersons since 1408. Lag Tower was the inspiration for the castle of Redgauntlet in the novel of the same name by Sir Walter Scott.

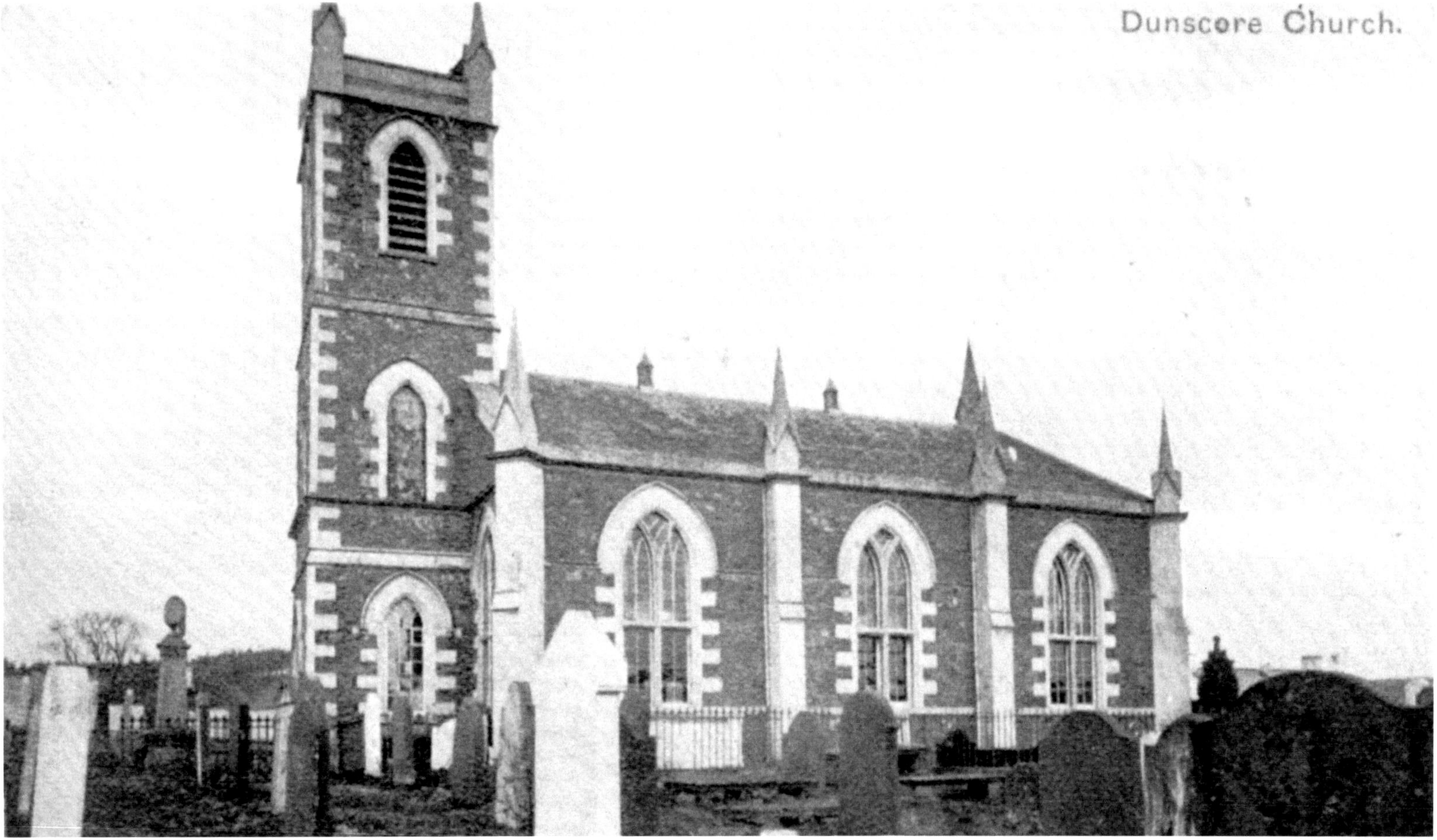


Dunscore Parish Church around 1909. The original place of Christian worship was situated south east of the parish around 1170 on land gifted to the Abbey of Holywood by monks from Melrose. The Old Dunscore Church was near the churchyard, but in 1649 a petition presented to the Scottish Parliament by James Grierson of Dalgonar sought to move the church because it had become a hazard. The petition was granted and so a church was built in the village. When that church fell into disrepair the present church was built in 1823 on the demolition site. It was designed in the Gothic style by James Thomson of Dumfries. It is made from whinstone and dressed sandstone, which was painted white around the doors and windows, as seen in the picture. In 2011 the paint was removed and the church restored to its former natural colour. A clock has since been added to the tower. The clock is in memory of a native of the district, Dr W A Ramsay (1937-1966), from his grateful patients. *Continued overleaf.*

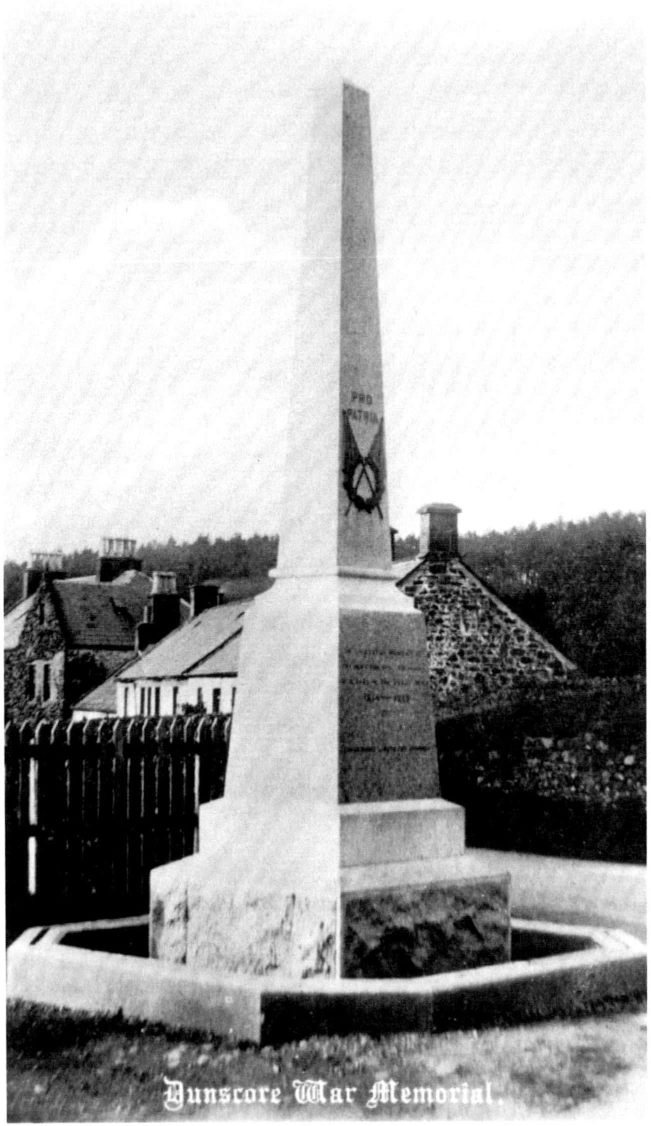


*Continued from previous page*: Inside is the old baptismal font, which had been built into the wall, but was taken out and made freestanding in 1923. When Craig Church closed in 1955, the memorial plaque to Jane Haining was removed from there and placed in this church. There is also a beautiful stained glass memorial to four of the congregation (William Cringean, John Fergusson, James Todd and William Wilson) who lost their lives in the First World War.

Close to the church is a memorial cairn and plaque dedicated to Jane Haining. Jane was born in 1897 at Lochanhead Farm near Dunscore and attended the village school and later Dumfries Academy where she was dux in 1915. She worshipped at the Craig Free Church in Dunscore and later at Queen's Park Church in Glasgow when she worked in the Coats thread factory in Paisley. Jane, having become interested in missionary work, then secured the post of matron of a Jewish Mission School in Budapest, Hungary in 1932.

Jane made a visit home in 1939 and then returned to work, but was soon advised by the Church leaders to come home because of the worsening conditions in Europe. Jane, however, steadfastly remained at her post taking care of her pupils, but when the Gestapo arrived at the mission in April 1944, she was arrested and charged with anti - Nazi offences, including working with Jews and weeping when seeing the girls in her care forced to wear the yellow star. She was eventually transported to Auschwitz and tattooed with the number 7946. She died there in July 1944. Exactly how no one knows. The official certificate sent to Edinburgh a month later stated "cachexia" ( general collapse of the system due to insufficient feeding) as the cause of death. Memorials to Jane are also to be found today in Budapest, Jerusalem, Glasgow and in Dunscore. In 1997 in memory of Jane, the Jewish award of Yad Vashem's Righteous of the Nations was given to her half sister, Mrs Agnes O' Brien.

Dunscore War Memorial. This red granite obelisk was constructed by Messrs Dodds and Son of Dumfries to commemorate the 40 men of Dunscore parish who died in the First World War and was unveiled in 1920 by Mrs Johnston of Stroquhan. After the Second World War a further nine names were added. The memorial sits at the junction of two roads in front of the house occupied by a Dr Morton who donated part of his garden for the site.

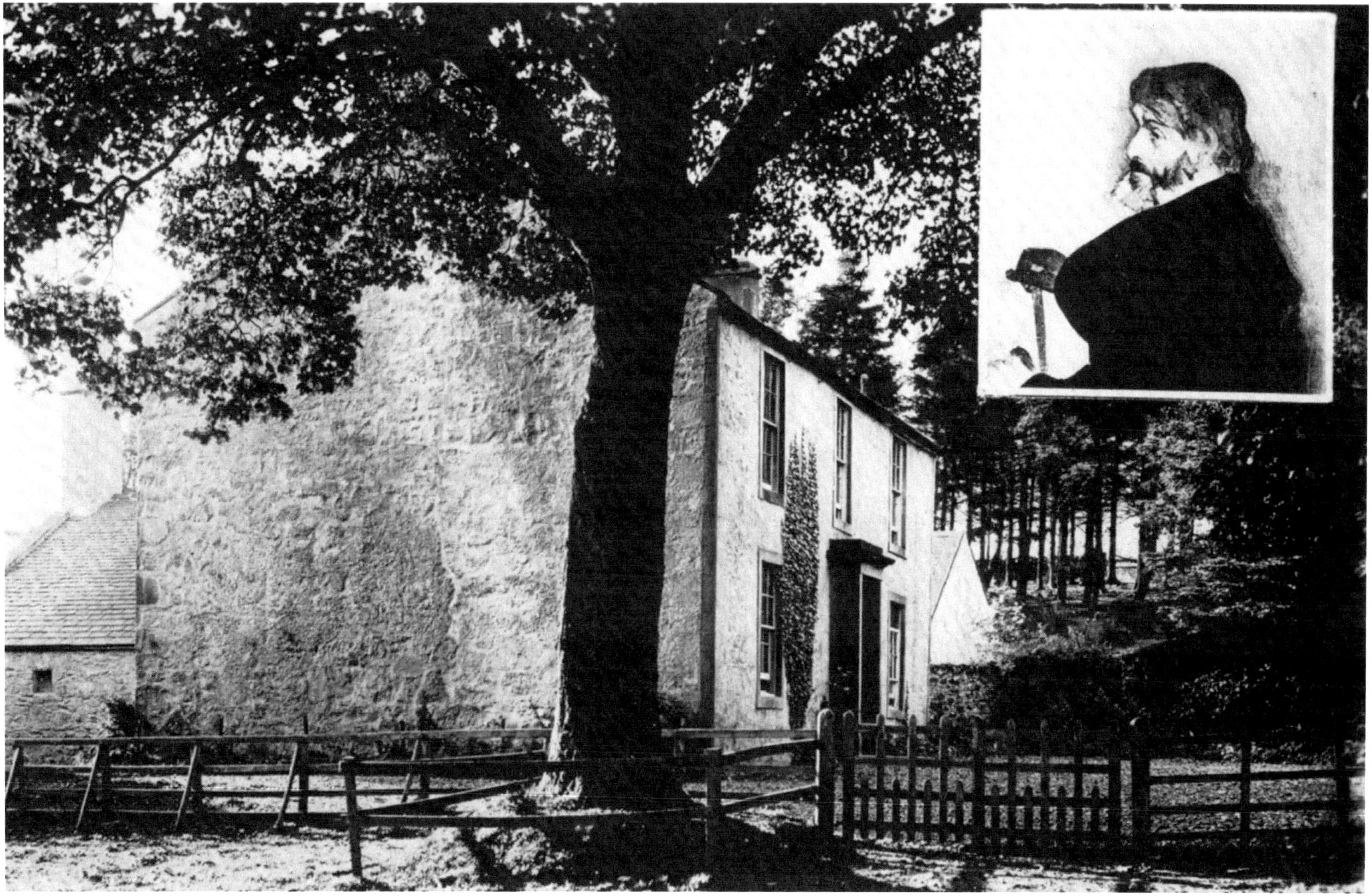

Craigenputtock Farm became the home of the Ecclefechan-born writer, Thomas Carlyle (inset picture) and his wife, Jane Welsh, from 1828 until 1834, before they moved to London. When Jane died in 1866, Thomas inherited the farm, from his in-laws, which he then bequeathed to Edinburgh University in order to endow bursaries. Carlyle's *Sartor Resartus* was written here along with his essay on Burns for the *Edinburgh Review*.

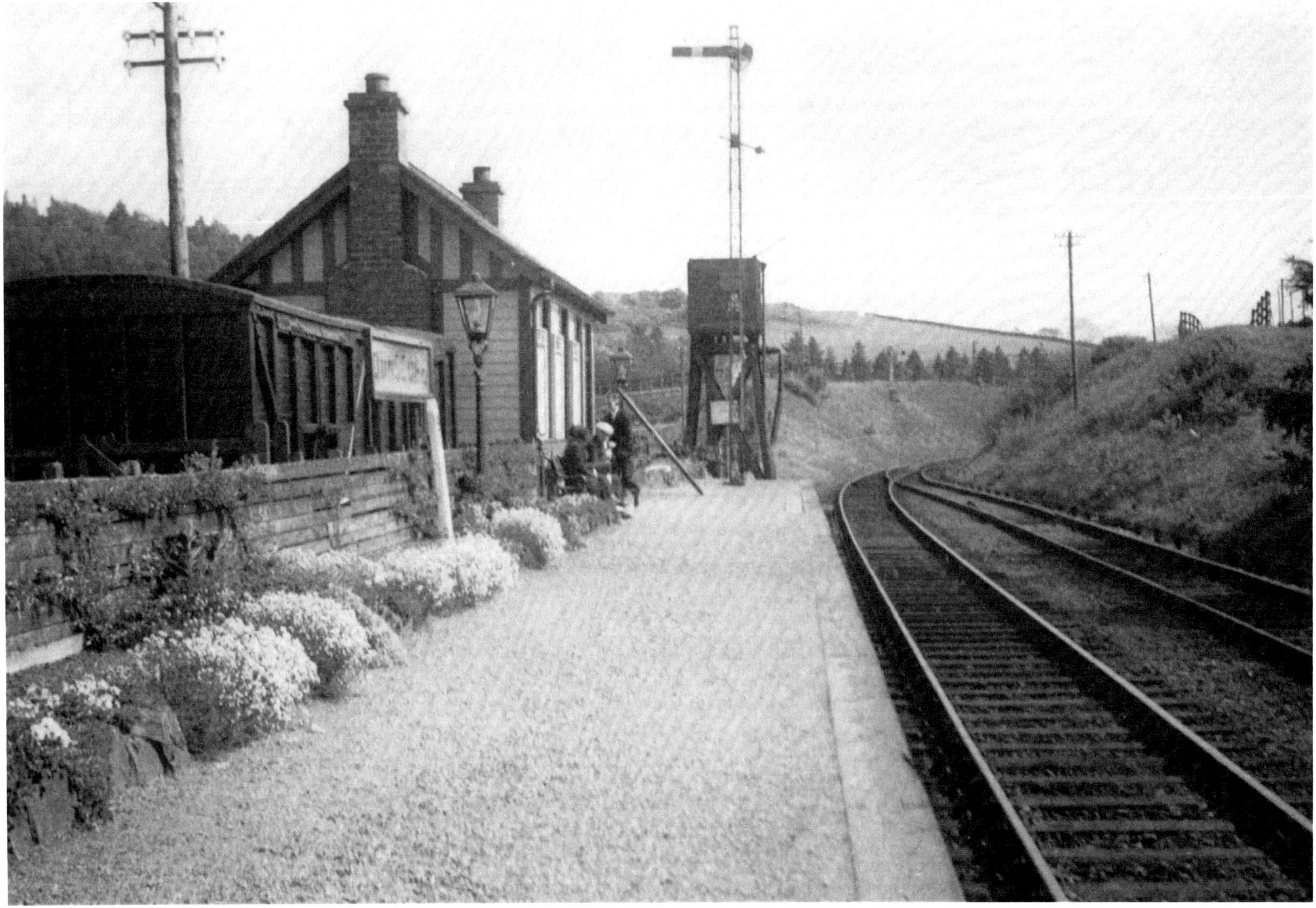

Dunscore Station usually had two services in each direction on weekdays with an additional service on Saturdays. The stationmaster in 1911 was John Scaife.

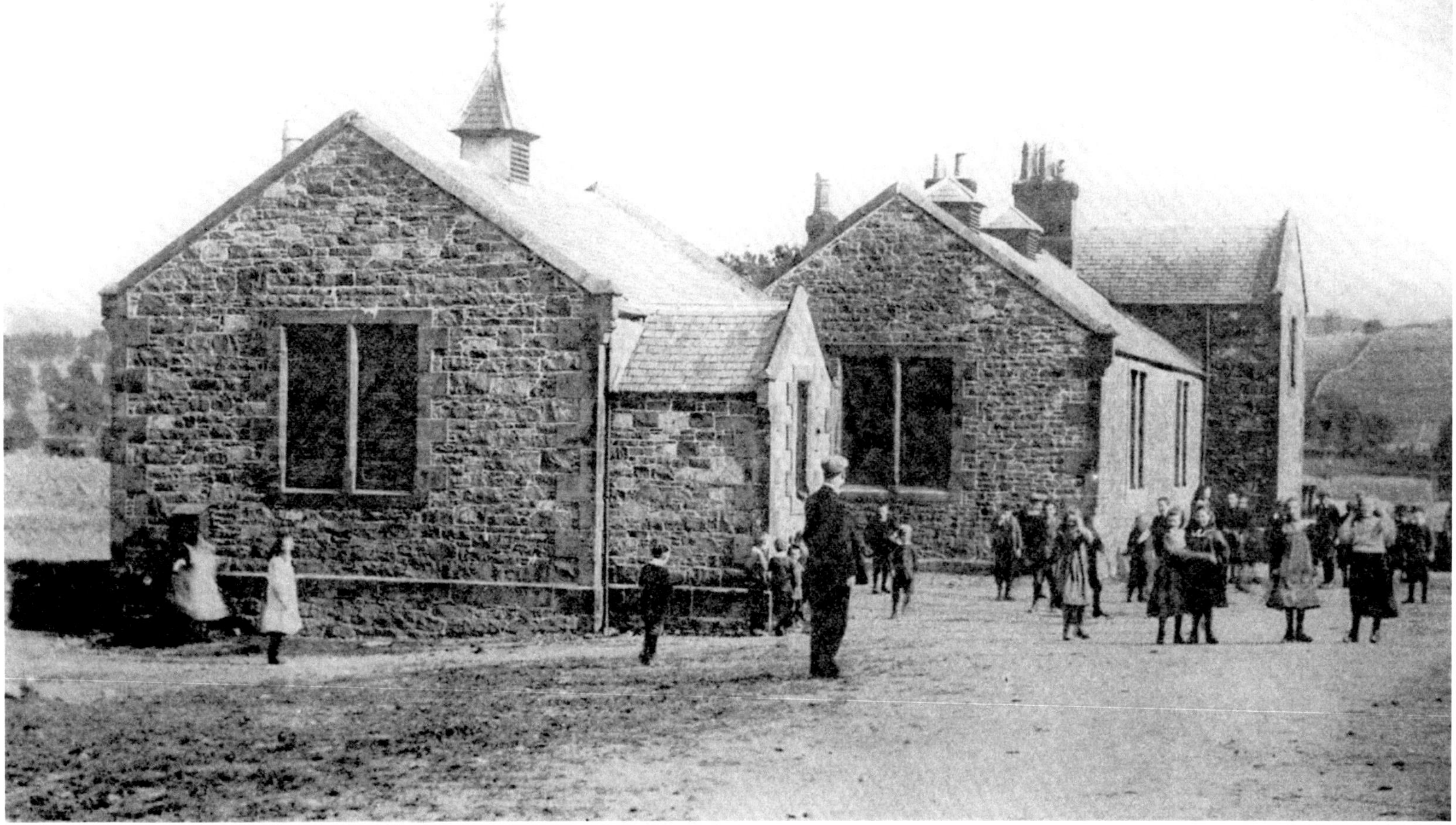

Dunscore Village School in 1904 when the schoolmaster was Daniel Gold. The school was closed in 1963, but is now used as a pre-school centre. A modern school has been built on its former playground.

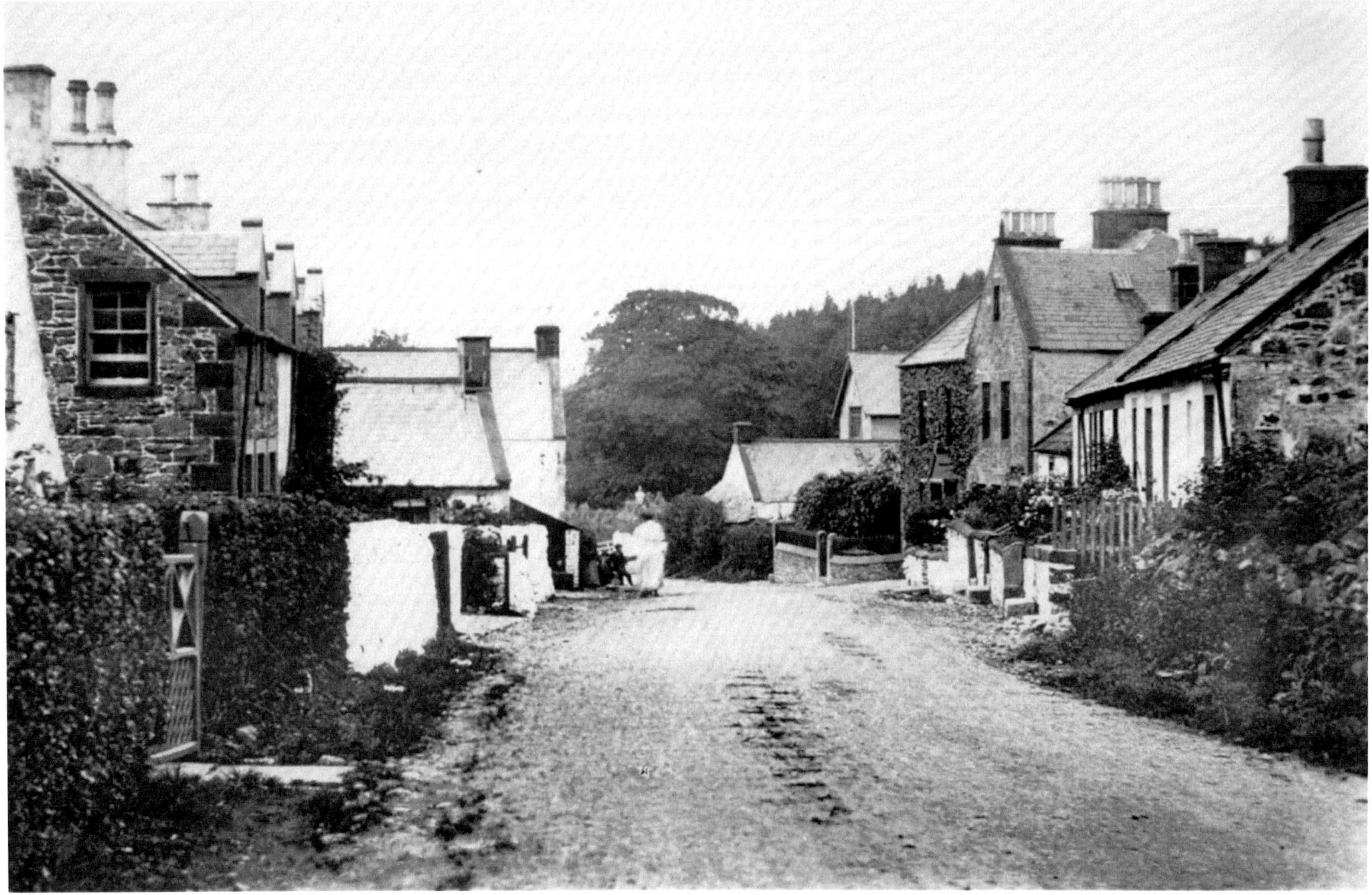

Dunscore Village – Main Street looking west – 1913. According to the street directory of 1911-12 Miller Irving ran the King's Arms Hotel; William Kirkpatrick was the bootmaker; grocers were D Miller and Mrs Kirk; the butcher was D Pagan; the constable was R McDonald; the Rev A Masterton was in the manse; Mrs Waugh ran the post office and Mrs Rae a lodging house.

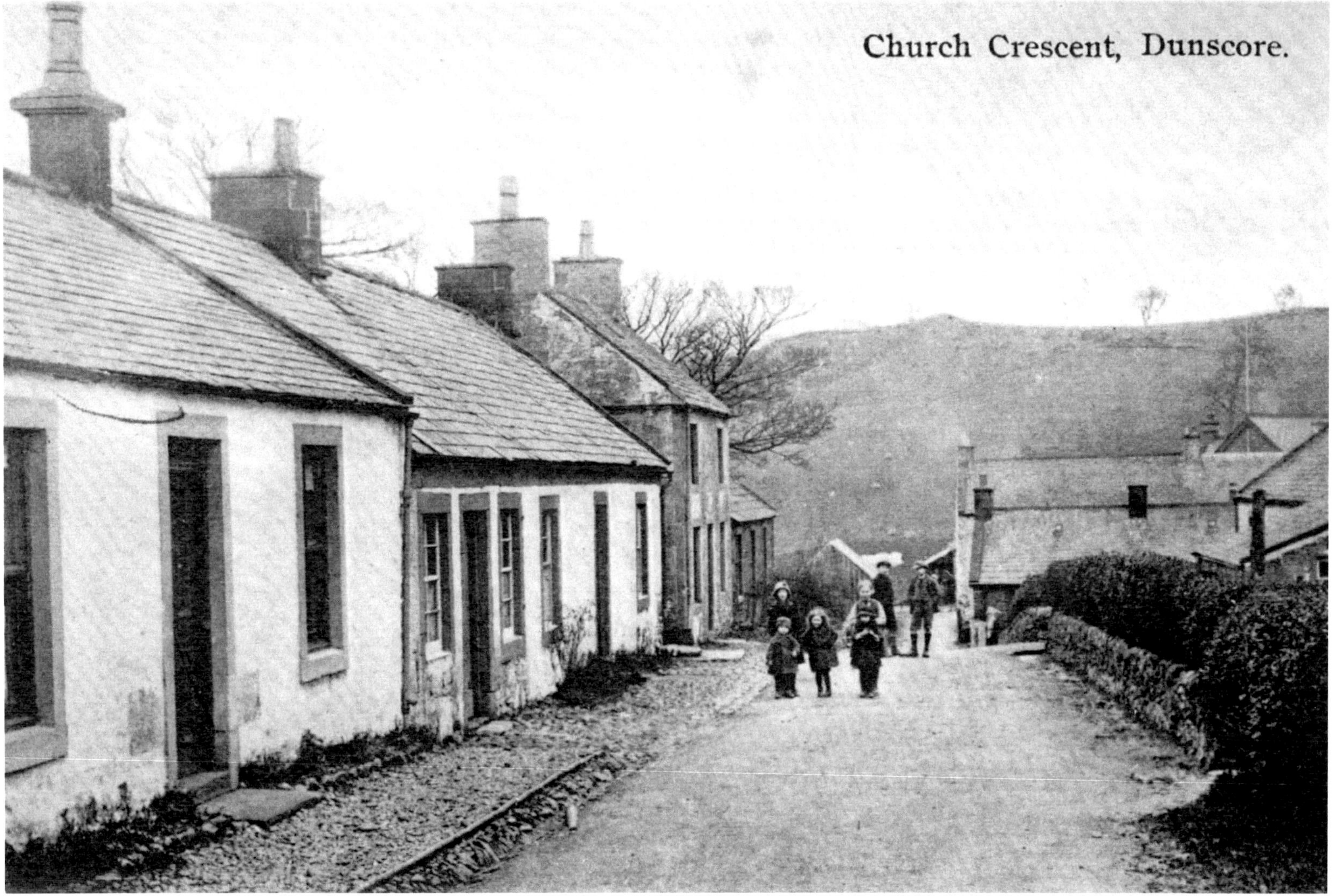


Church Crescent, Dunscore, looking down from the church. The village hall is situated off this street to the left. The population of Dunscore rose from 651 in 1755 to 1,578 in 1851, but has since declined.

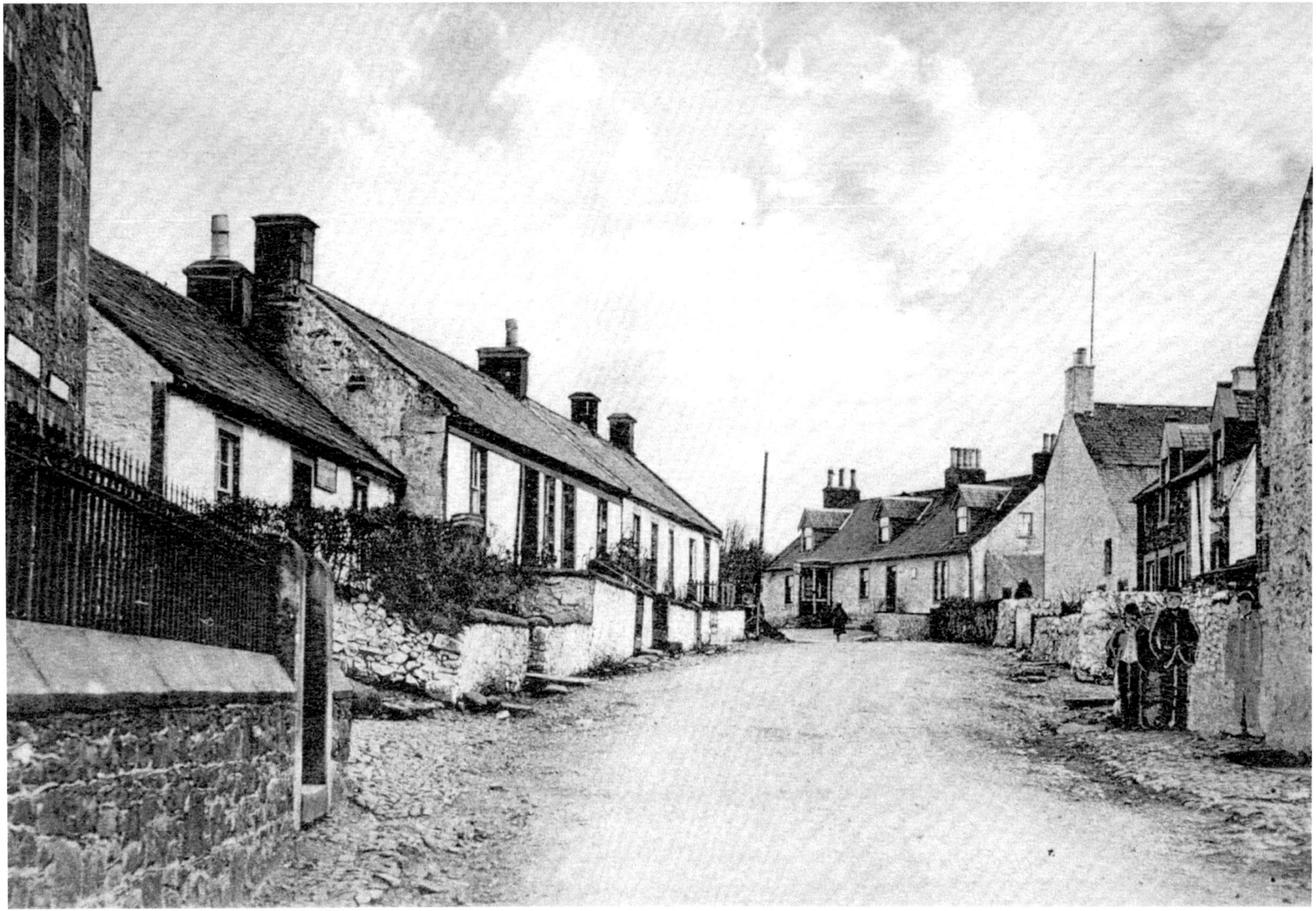

Dunscore on the road to Stroquhan. Note the drawings chalked on the wall on the right. The post office is on left.